Our American Century

A Century of Sports

★

By the Editors of Time-Life Books, Alexandria, Virginia

With a Foreword by Walter Iooss Jr.

Contents

★

Foreword

Sports. My childhood days were filled with sports. Stickball, football, basketball—I played them all. I covered the walls of my room with photographs cut out of sports magazines. In school I drew pictures of athletes, trying to depict the ballet of sport, sculpted bodies in striking positions.

Sports were my passion, but I could not yet imagine how that passion could be translated into my life's work. I never thought seriously about photography until, when I was 15, my father got season tickets to the Giants football games. He was a musician, not a photographer, but he liked to shoot pictures from the grandstand with a 300-millimeter telephoto lens. I was slow to take to it, but around midseason I had my first look, and it was a revelation. I discovered that life through a telephoto can look stunning, because you eliminate everything you don't want to see.

I was hooked on photography from that moment, and I started practicing, learning, improving. In 1961 *Sports Illustrated* published one of my pictures—a black-and-white shot of an 86-year-old man who had built a 33-foot sloop without blueprints, entirely by sight and feel. The magazine has been my employer, my psyche, my life ever since.

My subjects have included swimsuit models and Little Leaguers—I shot the picture on the title page in my hometown in 1965—but mostly they've been professional athletes: Bill Russell, Wilt Chamberlain, Joe Namath, Martina Navratilova, Cal Ripken Jr., Jackie Joyner-Kersee, Ken Griffey Jr., and a guy named Jordan, to name a few. I shot them as they created some of the memorable moments of the century.

As this book so richly shows, much has changed in the world of sports since I started. But the goal of sports photography remains the same: to control an image of an action or emotion. Controlling that image is what the gallery of my photographs on this and the following pages is all about. If you can position an athlete like Debi Thomas just where you want her, with the light just right, it's yours, and it's unique in all the world. The same can be said of the hundreds of wonderful images in this volume, created by countless photographers throughout the century, and augmented with exciting, informative commentary. Enjoy the moments.

Figure skater Debi Thomas etches a skein of patterns as she deftly whirls through a session on the ice in 1987. At Calgary the following year Thomas became the first African American medalist in a Winter Olympics.

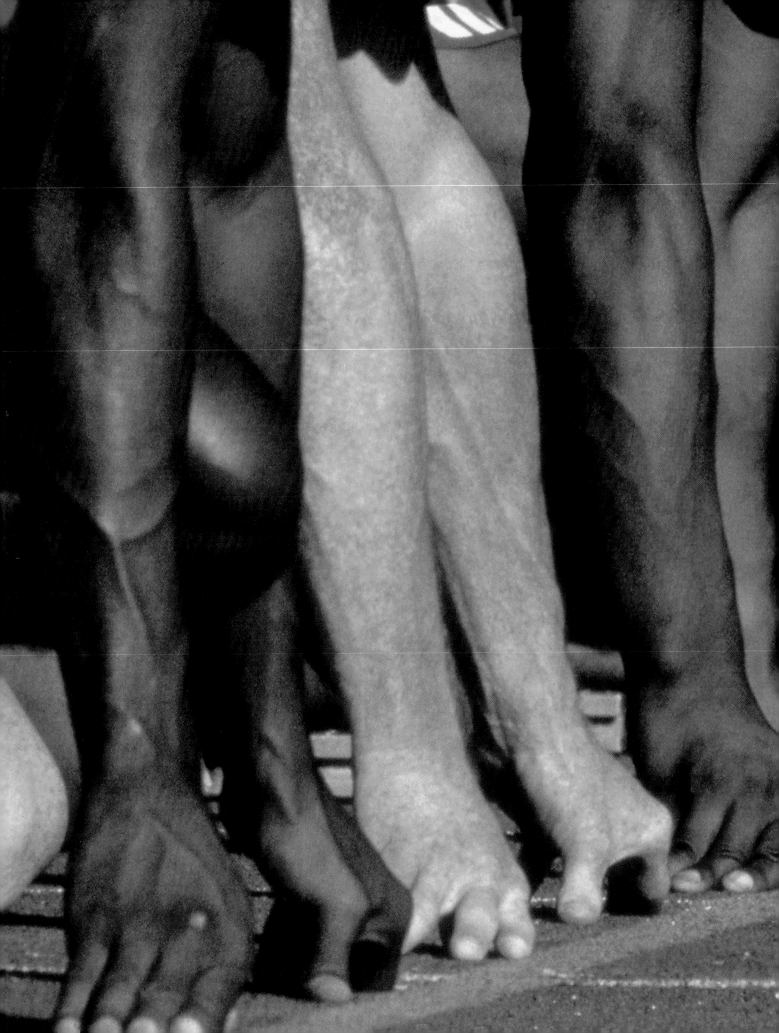

This curtain of arms of sprinters lined up for a dash in Los Angeles in 1983 marks a moment of extreme tension as the runners await the sound of the starter's pistol to send them exploding from the blocks.

In an image that defines the essence of fluid motion,
swimmer Todd Torres is captured an instant before
his head and shoulders will shatter the water's surface during a race at the Atlanta Olympics in 1996.

Flying dirt and helmet give vivid evidence of an attempt at a steal by Detroit's Alan Trammell in a 1993 game at Tiger Stadium. Oakland A's third baseman Craig Paquette applies the tag.

Tape, chalk, and steel bands of muscle are the tools
of gymnast Tim Daggett's trade. Daggett brought
it all together for a stunning perfect 10 on the high
bar at the Los Angeles Olympics in 1984.

A defender collides in midair with a ball carrier in a college football game. The scene, framed through a telephoto lens, combines the beauty of a still life with the drama of a train wreck.

All eyes bear witness to the soaring power and grace of modern-day basketball as the Portland Trail Blazers' Clyde "the Glide" Drexler puts on a show during a 1987 slam dunk contest.

Championship Century

★

100 YEARS OF HEROES

During a century bursting with record-shattering achievements in all forms of human endeavor, this moment stood out: On May 6, 1954, a 25-year-old English medical student named Roger Bannister ran a mile in 3 minutes 59.4 seconds *(left)*. This "tall, pale-skinned explorer of human exhaustion," as the first issue of *Sports Illustrated* described him, had crashed through one of the most formidable barriers in sports: the four-minute mile.

Bannister's feat, an ultimate test of courage, will, and ability, inspired athletes everywhere, but especially in the United States. Here, in the second half of the 20th century, sports of all kinds began to assume an importance unparalleled even in ancient Greece. Sports helped spur social change, providing unprecedented opportunity for heretofore excluded groups—women and African Americans like tennis champion Arthur Ashe *(inset)*, the first black man to win a major singles title. At the same time, television transformed sports into entertainment for the masses, allowing even couch potatoes to participate, albeit vicariously, in their favorite pastimes. Sports above all became big business, spawning myriad millionaires, including many of the players themselves.

The man voted the outstanding male athlete of the century's first 50 years was born

---

Incredulous timers check their watches as miler Roger Bannister cracks the four-minute barrier at Oxford in 1954. Two decades later, in 1975, tennis player Arthur Ashe (inset) cracked a color barrier at Wimbledon.

Jim Thorpe shows off a newly acquired skill—throwing the javelin—at a track meet in Carlisle, Pennsylvania, a few months before his remarkable performance at the 1912 Olympics.

Attired in a straw boater and bow tie in 1922, Babe Ruth stands among adoring young fans. "God himself" to children, as one sportswriter put it, the Babe always responded with gregarious good cheer, recalling his own days in an orphanage.

too early to share in the wealth. Native American Jim Thorpe *(left)* led the tiny Carlisle Indian School to victory over such collegiate football powers of his day as Harvard. Later he became America's first pro football star. He also played six years of Major League Baseball. But his most astonishing performances came during the 1912 Olympics in Stockholm, where he won both the decathlon and the pentathlon.

The titles earned him worldwide admiration and the praise of royalty. "Sir, you are the world's greatest athlete," Sweden's King Gustav told him. "Thanks, King," was Thorpe's snappy comeback. But then a newspaper revealed that Thorpe had violated the stringent and unforgiving requirements then in effect for holding amateur status. For a scarce few dollars a week he had spent two summers pitching and playing first base in a minor league in North Carolina. The practice was common among collegians, who usually eluded detection by using assumed names, but the naive Thorpe took no such precautions. He was compelled to give back his Olympic gold medals, and his name was erased from the record books. The pain of that loss never left him; neither medals nor records would be restored until 1982, nearly three decades after he died in poverty.

The Golden Age of Sport. Thorpe's athletic ability was waning just when sport entered what is generally considered its golden age, the 1920s. This era saw the emergence of a new breed of sporting hero, one celebrated not only in print but also in newsreels and on the radio. Babe Ruth *(left)*, Jack Dempsey, Red Grange, Bill Tilden, and Bobby Jones all became national celebrities. A boxing match in 1926 featuring Dempsey, the heavyweight champion, drew 120,000 spectators *(page 84)*—more than had ever attended any sporting event. But it was his friend the Babe—loud, brassy, "Ruthian" in his achievements and appetites—who personified the Roaring Twenties. The first star to hire a press agent and to earn as much outside a sport as in it, the Sultan of Swat slugged his way into the hearts of millions of Americans, most of whom had never set foot in a ballpark.

The titan of tennis, "Big Bill" Tilden *(opposite, top right),* was not all that big—6 feet 1 and 155 pounds—but he played with a power, grace, and flair not previously seen. A late bloomer, he couldn't make the varsity tennis team at the University of Pennsylvania when he was 20, but he won seven U.S. Open championships and claimed the honor of being the first American man to take a Wimbledon title.

Bobby Jones *(right, bottom)* bloomed early, winning his first major golf championship in 1923 at age 21. Known for his wit and courtesy, the talented Georgian brushed aside praise for his honesty when he once assessed himself penalty strokes even though no one else had noticed the inadvertent technical violation. "You might as well praise a man for not robbing a bank," he said. In all, Jones won 13 of the 21 major tournaments he competed for. In 1930 he became the only man in golf history to win a Grand Slam—the open and amateur titles in both the United States and Britain—and was accorded a ticker-tape parade in New York City. Then, at age 28 he stunned everyone by retiring. He practiced law and helped found the Augusta National Golf Club and a tournament so prestigious it is known simply as the Masters.

A child of the golden age, Mildred Didrikson *(inset)* could hit a baseball so far as a teenager that her awed male teammates nicknamed her Babe. In an era when female athletes were a genteel oddity, Didrikson dared to be flamboyant and foul-mouthed. She excelled at every sport she tried—basketball, tennis, swimming, bowling, billiards, even boxing—and loved to brag about it. Asked if there was anything she didn't play, she replied, "Yeah, dolls."

The female Babe first made national headlines in the 1932 Olympics in Los Angeles. Only 21, she won gold in the javelin throw and the 80-meter hurdles and missed first place in the high jump only because of a style technicality. For a career, she finally settled on golf, capturing 56 major tournaments and helping to establish the Ladies Professional Golf Association. She accounted for her prodigious drives by explaining, "You've got to loosen your girdle and let her rip!" One of the most versatile athletes ever, she vanquished the widely held opinion that women were too frail—or else too ladylike—for competitive sports.

Bill Tilden reaches for a one-handed backhand that, like his long white pants and white shirt, was standard early in the century. Below, elegant in knickers and sweater, Bobby Jones follows through on a shot with his hickory-shafted wood en route to victory in the 1930 British Open. Babe Didrikson (left) clutches a leather basketball with the same sure hands—she once scored 104 points in a high-school game—that later allowed her to dominate women's golf.

Her face a picture of concentration, Althea Gibson connects with a forehand in 1957 on her way to becoming the first black women's singles champion at Wimbledon. "I'm just another tennis player," she said, "not a Negro tennis player."

Beaded hair flying, the Williams sisters—Venus (above) and Serena (right)—show their flair and fierce competitive drive. Venus won all three of their face-to-face encounters on the pro tour, but Serena captured the big one—the 1999 U.S. Open. The sisters were inseparable off the court. "We have two separate hearts," said Venus, "at least I think so."

Breaking the Color Barrier. Professional sports, like much of American society, was mostly segregated for nearly half the century. The principal exception was boxing, where both Jack Johnson *(page 83)* and Joe Louis *(page 87)* had reigned as world heavyweight champions. In track and field, Jesse Owens competed against and defeated all comers. His astonishing haul of four gold medals in the 1936 Olympics in Berlin *(page 167)* would be unequaled for nearly five decades. But after embarrassing Adolf Hitler and giving the lie to his delusions about a "master race," Owens came home to the same racism that had plagued his country even before he pulled on an Olympic uniform.

At midcentury sports became a central arena in the struggle for civil rights, a showcase for racial change. In 1947 Jackie Robinson became Major League Baseball's first black player *(page 42)*, opening a crack in the color barrier that other ballplayers then passed through. Two years later he won the National League's Most Valuable Player award. Those who followed him during the next decade owed an unpayable debt to a man who walked through the fire of racial hatred for them. One was the incomparable Willie Mays *(inset, opposite)*, who never lost appreciation for his predecessor. "Every time I look at my pocketbook," Mays said, "I see Jackie Robinson."

That breakthrough in baseball created a powerful ripple effect in other American sports. Jim Brown *(opposite, top right)*, arguably the greatest runner in NFL history, was not the first black player in pro football, but he carried himself with a militant pride that tolerated no racist echoes from the bad old days.

The debut of Bill Russell in 1956 underscored the dramatic impact of desegregation in the National Basketball Association. Russell led the Boston Celtics to 11 championships in 13 years *(pages 104-106)*, and in 1966, while still a player, he became the Celtics' coach and the first African American to manage in big-league sports. Major League Baseball would not have a black manager until 1974; the National Football League would not have a black coach until 1989. Barriers of both race and class crumbled under the powerful tennis strokes of Althea Gibson *(left, top)*. The tall, lean daughter of a sharecropper, Gibson was born on a South Carolina cotton farm and grew up in Harlem, where she played paddleball on the baked asphalt of West 143rd Street. Tired of high school, she dropped out to work as a coffee shop counter girl, elevator operator, and chicken plucker in a poultry-processing factory.

The place where tennis traditionally flourished, the country club, admitted neither blacks nor working-class players. Gibson took up tennis under the auspices of a hopeful and nurturing black organization called the American Tennis Association. She was gifted with natural ability and an attitude. "I'd knock you down if you got in the way," she said later. "I just wanted to play my best."

Both paid off in 1950, when she became the first black player—male or female—invited to the previously lily-white tournaments of the U.S. Lawn Tennis Association. Seven years later she won the women's singles both at Wimbledon and at the U.S. Nationals at Forest Hills. She repeated both triumphs the following year, but her hard-won celebrity still did not count for much with many Americans. At the top of her game, she was denied a room at leading hotels. The famous Pump Room of Chicago's Ambassador East Hotel even refused to book reservations for a luncheon in her honor.

Fortunately, much has improved since then. But tennis fans looking for a second African American woman to become a Grand Slam singles champion had a long wait. Then 17-year-old Serena Williams *(opposite, inset),* playing in the stadium named for Arthur Ashe at New York's National Tennis Center, won the 1999 U.S. Open and boldly set her sights on additional Grand Slam titles, such as Wimbledon. "I can see myself lifting that plate for sure," she said, referring to the English trophy. "I just can't see it not happening." Her confidence—and that of her equally talented older sister Venus *(opposite, bottom left)*— reminded fans of Muhammad Ali *(far right).*

Heavyweight champion Ali never knew his "place." With a wit as quick as his fists and the courage of his convictions, he put an end to that era—described by the novelist Joyce Carol Oates—"in which the

Willie Mays follows the flight of a ball he blasted in 1958 during spring training. No one else had ever combined such power at the plate, speed on the base paths, and defensive brilliance.

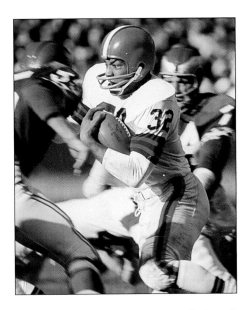

Holding the ball tightly, Jim Brown bulls through two Philadelphia Eagles. A defender said that the experience was like "tackling a locomotive." After nine years of setting records for the Cleveland Browns, Brown retired at age 30.

All sweat and sweetness, Muhammad Ali smiles for the camera of Neil Leifer. He billed himself as "the Greatest" and hyped his championship bouts with poetry that presaged the lyrics of rap music.

black athlete was given to know that his presence was provisional and not a right." During the 1960s he was the nation's most controversial athlete. People derided him for joining the Nation of Islam, changing his name, and refusing induction into the army during the Vietnam War—"No Vietcong," he said, "ever called me nigger." Decades later he would be the best-known, most-revered athlete on earth.

The Impact of Television. Newspapers, radio, and magazines played a prominent role in the burgeoning place of sports in American culture. But it was the advent of widespread TV coverage that transformed athletics into a kind of national religion—the true opiate of the masses. Tens of millions of sports fans, even those who had never purchased a ticket for a game of any kind, could now witness moments of high drama and inspiration without ever leaving home.

Arnold Palmer (left) follows through at the 1962 Masters, and Jack Nicklaus studies a putt at the 1980 U.S. Open. Palmer was the most-beloved golfer of the century, Nicklaus the best of all time. "You learn how to win by winning," said Nicklaus. "As long as I'm prepared, I always expect to win."

The happy confluence of the TV camera and Arnold Palmer's swashbuckling charisma converted the elitist game of golf into a spectator sport during the late 1950s. Galleries and TV viewers alike could identify with Palmer's down-home style *(far left, top)*. He had a muscular frame, tousled hair, and shirttails that flapped in the breeze. He hitched his pants, shamelessly showed his emotions, and wisecracked with the large following of fans who came to be known as Arnie's Army. No player had ever inspired so many ordinary people not only to watch golf but also to take up the game. His penchant for charging from behind further endeared him to his army and the networks. Palmer won 60 pro tournaments—not the least of them four Masters championships.

In the 1962 U.S. Open, Palmer confronted a 22-year-old rookie who would be his greatest rival. Rumpled looking, wearing a funny hat, and so chubby his fellow pros had nicknamed him Ohio Fats, Jack Nicklaus *(near left, top)* played with such detachment he could go an entire round without speaking a word. But he stunned Arnie and his army by coolly capturing the Open by three strokes in a head-to-head play-off. With a combination of finesse, smarts, and booming drives that typically carried

Billie Jean King reaches for a backhand at Wimbledon. Martina Navratilova said of King's efforts on behalf of women athletes, "She was a crusader fighting a battle for all of us."

285 yards, Nicklaus won the Masters six times—among a career total of 20 major championships—and earned a reputation as the greatest golfer ever. After watching him score a record 271 in the 1965 Masters, Bobby Jones remarked, "Palmer . . . played superbly, but Nicklaus played a game with which I am not familiar."

Through TV, Carl Lewis (right) was cheered by millions when he won four gold medals at the Los Angeles Olympics in 1984, duplicating Jesse Owens's 48-year-old feat. In the latter part of his 41-year career, horse racing's legendary Bill Shoemaker (right, middle), who rode to victory a record 8,833 times, became a familiar household figure via the TV screen. Thanks to television and the Brazilian star Pelé (inset, below), even soccer—the most popular team sport in the world but then foreign to most Americans—began to flourish in the United States in the 1980s.

When Billie Jean King (opposite, bottom left) was 12, she vowed to herself, "If I ever become a great champion, I'll change tennis." She did both. Women's singles champion at Wimbledon six times and at the U.S. Open four times, she took a total of 39 titles in Grand Slam tournaments. "When in doubt," a sportswriter observed of her aggressive style, "she charged." That also proved true off the court, where she fought for gender equity in sports. She helped launch the first women's pro tour and establish the principle of equal prize money for women. She also started a foundation and a magazine devoted to women's sports. But her most famous achievement came in 1973 in the much ballyhooed "Battle of the Sexes" in the Houston Astrodome. Before a national television audience, she whipped Bobby Riggs, a 55-year-old former champion and self-proclaimed "male chauvinist pig," in three straight sets. It was a turning point in the public's acceptance of female athletes.

Following in King's wake were superstar Chris Evert and her even more accomplished rival, Martina Navratilova (inset, opposite), who had defected from Commu-

A blur of classic form, Carl Lewis runs up to the takeoff for the long jump at the 1984 Olympics in Los Angeles. Lewis competed in four Olympics, garnering nine gold medals, and would most likely have won more but for the U.S. boycott of the Moscow Games in 1980.

Retiring as the winningest jockey ever, Bill Shoemaker poses after one of his 40,350 races. In December 1999 Shoemaker was on hand at Hollywood Park in California as his 24-year-old record was eclipsed by his friend, 52-year-old Laffit Pincay Jr.

Soccer immortal Edson Arantes do Nascimento—better known as Pelé—celebrates a goal in 1975. Officially a national treasure in Brazil, he was lured out of retirement by a three-year, $4.75-million offer to play for the New York Cosmos.

Wearing his trademark cowboy hat, wraparound sunglasses, and smile, Richard Petty relaxes before the running of the 1987 Daytona 500. As always, his car was emblazoned with the number 43 and painted a color known as "Petty blue."

The Edmonton Oilers' Wayne Gretzky moves the puck toward the New York Islanders' goal in the 1983 Stanley Cup finals. "What he does on the ice isn't taught," said his coach. "It comes straight down from the Lord."

Pete Sampras stretches for a graceful backhand volley at Wimbledon, where he won six of his record-tying 12 Grand Slam singles titles. Only the great Australian player Roy Emerson won as many.

nist Czechoslovakia in 1975. Sportswriter Frank Deford described Navratilova as "the other, the odd one, alone: left-hander in a right-handed universe, gay in a straight world; defector, immigrant." With her wicked serve and ferocious volleys, she captured nine singles titles at Wimbledon and won more matches and tournaments than any other pro, male or female. She was the first female athlete to earn more than one million dollars in a year. Just as impressive, she possessed the courage at the height of her success in 1981 to address a subject that had lurked in the shadows, making a public announcement of her sexual orientation.

Show Business, Big Business. Sonny Werblin, the one-time owner of the New York Jets, articulated an innovative truth during the 1960s. "Football," he announced, "is show business." So, it turned out, were myriad other sports, from auto racing to volleyball. Pumped up by television exposure and revenues, lucrative luxury boxes, and merchandising deals for caps, jackets, and jerseys, they were also big business. Big-league franchises of every kind multiplied, and cities offered to build dream stadiums in hopes they would come. Franchises soared in value; in 1999 the Washington Redskins football team sold for $800 million, and such prestigious franchises as the New York Yankees probably could bring a billion dollars. Even in nominally amateur spheres such as college football and basketball, a bowl or tournament appearance might be worth millions to the institution.

Pro performers shared the largess. Like other major-leaguers, NBA players once needed to moonlight in the off-season to sustain themselves. By 1999 the average NBA salary had soared to $2.9 million, and some 50 players earned more than $5 million. The biggest earners were those who not only ranked with the best in their game but also possessed the popular appeal to reap celebrity endorsements. Arnold Palmer became the first athlete to establish a multimillion-dollar empire of endorsements and enterprises that traded on his name. But the biggest of them all was basketball star Michael Jordan *(opposite, top)*. He was described by popular historian David Halberstam as "not just the ultimate basketball player; he is the ultimate show." By endorsing sneakers, underwear, batteries, long-distance telephone service, and other products, Jordan made some $78 million—less than half of it in salary—during his final year with the Chicago Bulls *(pages 120-123)*.

Though richly compensated in tournament prize money, the dominant male tennis player of the 1990s, Pete Sampras *(inset, opposite)*, was judged to lack sufficient panache and style to "be like Mike" and really cash in. But as the winner of a record-tying 12 Grand Slam singles titles, he showed that he was one of a handful of elite athletes who deserved to be counted with Jordan among the century's true champions.

Richard Petty *(opposite, top)*, ruler of stock-car racing for 35 years, was another. By both the force of his skill behind the wheel and his laid-back personality, the lanky driver from Level Cross, North Carolina, took the sport off the small-town dirt tracks of its early days and made it into one of the biggest spectator sports in America, attracting huge crowds and rich TV contracts. The fans who idolized "King Richard" knew he gave the sport everything he could. He suffered concussions, broken toes, and a broken back, lost much of his hearing to the roar of the engine, and had 40 percent of his ulcer-ravaged stomach surgically removed. He always had a smile, some good-old-boy small talk, and an autograph for anyone who asked.

When Wayne Gretzky *(opposite, middle)* skated into the National Hockey League in 1978, few could have predicted that his impact on hockey would rival Petty's on auto racing. He was a skinny 17-year-old from Brantford, Ontario, who did not look strong enough or fast enough to make it. Yet with grace and awesome ice presence, he led the Edmonton Oilers to four Stanley Cups. Over a career of 20 seasons "the Great One" shattered practically every league record for goals and assists. Traded to Los Angeles in 1988, Gretzky helped hockey break through in new markets on the West Coast and in the Sun Belt. He also changed the sport's very image. No longer seen as a game for rowdy goons, it sparkled with the dazzling quickness and offensive creativity that was the legacy of the best player in hockey history.

Jackie Joyner-Kersee *(right)* did much the same for the world of running, jumping, javelin throwing, and other Olympic events. At her birth in 1962 in a little shack in East St. Louis, Illinois, her grandmother suggested she be named Jacqueline after the wife of President John F. Kennedy. "Someday," she said, "this girl will be the first lady of something." As it turned out, she became the first lady of track and field and

Michael Jordan cries tears of joy after leading the Chicago Bulls to their first NBA title in 1991. Probably basketball's best player ever and certainly its greatest showman, Jordan generated history's highest-flying highlight films and got to hug five more championship trophies.

Jackie Joyner-Kersee soars in the long jump at the 1996 Olympics in Atlanta. Forced out of the heptathlon by an injured right thigh, she went from sixth place to third on her final attempt in the long jump, ensuring a record sixth medal.

Football's Bo Jackson (above) carries the ball for the Los Angeles Raiders in 1990. Baseball's Bo Jackson (below) hits the ball for the Kansas City Royals in 1989. He was the only player ever selected for the All-Star Game in both sports.

one of the best woman athletes ever. Overcoming poverty as well as severe asthma and allergies that took her breath away, she garnered six medals in four Olympics—more than any other American woman in track and field. Her specialties were the long jump and the heptathlon, a grueling seven-event competition demanding speed, strength, and stamina. "Her performances are like a great opera or concert," said Bob Kersee, her coach and husband. "I feel like I should be wearing a tux when I watch them."

Observers expressed similar sentiments when they watched Bo Jackson, a man so gifted that he starred in two different major-league sports. Jackson was a devastating running back for the Los Angeles Raiders *(left)* and a hard-hitting outfielder for the Kansas City Royals *(left, bottom)*. "I once vowed I would never miss a Bo Jackson at bat," said his Royals teammate George Brett, "because whenever he bats, you never know what you're going to see that you've never seen before."

No one, not even Jim Thorpe, matched his performances. From 1987 through 1990 he was one of the most-feared batters in the American League. Once he slugged three home runs in a row. In the autumn, after baseball season ended, he took to the gridiron, twice uncorking touchdown runs of 90 yards or more from scrimmage. Although he was so shy in college that he stammered, his exploits made him the star of a famous series of hilarious television commercials that presented him as "the world's greatest athlete," gave the phrase "Bo knows" a place in everyday vernacular—and put him in line to earn almost seven million dollars in 1991.

But the gods say, *"Sic transit gloria mundi"* ("So passes away the glory of the world"), a sad truth that applies to athletes sooner than to most celebrities. Sports greatness is as vulnerable as the athlete's body, even a body as nearly perfect as that of Bo Jackson. In January 1991 he was tackled hard in a Raiders play-off game and suffered a severe injury to his left hip. In an eye-blink his ability to play football was ended, and his baseball career would never be the same. Waived to the Chicago White Sox, he struggled through 23 games the following spring before submitting to surgery to replace his ruined hip. Amazingly, he came back. He socked a home run in his very first at bat with his artificial hip and played valiantly through two seasons with it before retiring to complete his college education and enjoy his family.

Showdown on the 17th Hole. It was a historic confrontation that bridged nearly a century of American golf. In 1913 a 20-year-old former caddy and self-taught American amateur, Francis Ouimet *(inset),* defeated Britain's two best professionals in a play-off to win the U.S. Open. His stunning upset stirred American interest in a sport that had been considered primarily a British game. The scene of Ouimet's triumph was The Country Club in Brookline, Massachusetts, and the keys to it were a pair of timely putts on the 17th hole, which happened to be just across the street from the modest home where Ouimet grew up.

Fast-forward to near the end of the century. In September 1999 on the same course, teams of leading professionals from the United States and Europe met in the gentlemanly grudge match known as the Ryder Cup. Heading into the final day's play, the Americans were down by four points. No team had ever overcome a deficit of more than half that. But the Americans staged an extraordinary comeback that was culminated on the same 17th hole where Francis Ouimet had sparkled 86 years before. Justin Leonard, a 27-year-old Texan, did the improbable by sinking a 45-foot putt to clinch the U.S. victory *(right, top).*

The most prominent member of the U.S. team was Eldrick "Tiger" Woods *(right, middle).* Woods became the youngest Masters champion in history at age 21 when he won in 1997 by a record margin with a record low score. Long off the tee, deadly from the bunkers, with a deft putting stroke, Woods took his second major, the PGA, and seven other tournaments in 1999 and showed strong promise of someday displacing Jack Nicklaus as the best golfer of all time. Woods was also a symbol of America as melting pot. He calculated his ethnicity as one-fourth black, one-eighth Caucasian, one-eighth American Indian, one-fourth Thai, and one-fourth Chinese. Fans in an ethnically diverse nation could argue the relative merits of Woods and other favorite athletes without regard to class, race, or gender. For both participants and followers, sports in the 20th century reflected the great shared experience of American democracy.

Casting aside golf etiquette, members of the U.S. Ryder Cup team surge onto the 17th green at The Country Club in Brookline, Massachusetts, in 1999, to celebrate Justin Leonard's 45-foot putt that climaxed a record-breaking U.S. comeback.

Teammates, fellow Masters champions, and close friends, Tiger Woods (left) and Mark O'Meara make merry after the stunning U.S. Ryder Cup victory in 1999. For the Americans it was the 25th Cup win in 33 matches dating back to 1927.

Unheralded young Francis Ouimet (left) became the first American golf hero. His upset win in the 1913 U.S. Open ignited enthusiasm for the game across the country.

The National
Pastime

★

ETERNAL DRAMA OF THE DIAMOND

N o American sport can match baseball's legacy. Even before the Civil War the poet Walt Whitman dubbed it "the American game." As early as 1903 an agreement between the upstart American League and the 27-year-old National League led to the first World Series—between the Pittsburgh Pirates and the Boston Pilgrims (later the Red Sox)—and laid the foundation for the modern game.

Baseball's popularity soared. In 1910 President William Howard Taft, attending the Washington Senators' opening game, started an annual ritual by throwing out the first ball. A new tune—"Take Me Out to the Ball Game" —became the anthem of the sport, and fans flocked to the Chicago Cubs' Weeghman Park (later Wrigley Field), the Red Sox' Fenway Park, and other shiny new stadiums to cheer heroes like Cy Young, Honus Wagner, Napoleon Lajoie, Christy Mathewson, and Walter Johnson *(page 34, top left)*.

It was a rough-and-tumble era of scuffed balls and fistfights, and its towering figure was a snarling Georgian named Ty Cobb *(left)*, who joined the Detroit Tigers in 1905 as a 19-year-old outfielder. His nickname, the Georgia Peach, belied Cobb's essence: a malignant personality and a ferocious will to be first in everything. He mostly was. Using a unique batting style—he held the bat well above the nobbed end with hands spread wide apart—Cobb

Ty Cobb slides hard into third base in a game against the New York Highlanders (later renamed the Yankees) in 1909. Players said that Cobb would cut the legs off his own grandmother if she tried to tag him out.

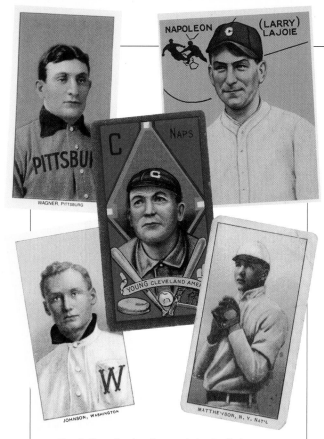

Baseball cards of early stars helped sell cigarettes as well as popularize the game.

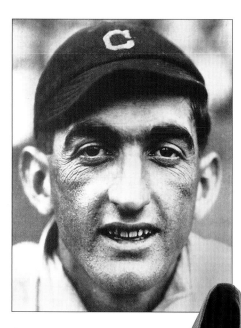

At right, Shoeless Joe Jackson's shoes. According to legend, Jackson got his nickname for playing the outfield barefoot in the minor leagues when his spikes were too tight.

sprayed hits everywhere. He led the American League in batting 12 times, on three occasions going over .400. When he retired after the 1928 season, he owned more than 90 records. Although many have since been broken, Cobb's .367 lifetime batting average remains all but unassailable.

Not only was Cobb the best player of his era, he was also the most hated. Asked why he was so combative, a teammate said: "He was still fighting the Civil War. As far as he was concerned, we were all damn Yankees." In New York in 1912, when a fan taunted him as a "half-nigger," Cobb vaulted the railing and stomped the man with his spiked shoes. The deed earned Cobb a suspension, which led his team to launch a short-lived strike and club management to hire as subs anybody who, in a cynical journalist's words, "could stop a grapefruit from rolling uphill."

After the United States entered World War I in 1917, baseball obeyed the national slogan Work or Fight. More than 225 players enlisted, including Cobb, Mathewson, and Tris Speaker. (Pitcher Mathewson, exposed to poison gas, died seven years later.) The 1918 season was cut back from 154 to 128 games, and "The Star-Spangled Banner" was played at a ball game for the first time, giving birth to a new tradition.

Baseball survived the war only to face a more sinister threat. In 1920 eight members of the Chicago White Sox were accused of selling out to gamblers and throwing the previous year's World Series to the underdog Cincinnati Reds. Although a jury acquitted them, all eight were banned for life by Commissioner Kenesaw Mountain Landis, an uncompromising former federal judge hired by the owners to restore the game's integrity.

One of the banned players was "Shoeless Joe" Jackson (left), an illiterate South Carolinian who was recognized as the best natural hitter of his day. A sportswriter described Jackson as "pure country, a wide-eyed gullible yokel," and his actual role, if any, in the plot remains unclear, as he led Series hitters with a .375 average and fielded flawlessly. When a tearful newsboy tugged on Jackson's arm and intoned, "Say it ain't so, Joe," he spoke for a disillusioned nation—and added a colorful phrase to Americana.

Baseball's Recovery, Boston's Curse. In 1920 Red Sox owner Harry Frazee was deeply in debt from bad investments on Broadway. To raise money, he sold his best player, George Herman "Babe" Ruth (right), to the New York Yankees. The Yankees at the time were baseball nobodies, while the Red Sox owned five World Series championships—more than any other club. After that deal the Yankees went on to build a dynasty unequaled in all

A youthful and still flat-bellied Babe Ruth sits in the Yankee dugout. His booming bat and outgoing personality resurrected baseball after the Black Sox scandal of 1919 and made him the most-beloved hero in all of sports.

The Dean brothers, Paul ("Daffy") at left, Dizzy at right, accounted for all four St. Louis wins in the 1934 World Series against Detroit. During the regular season, Dizzy won 30, Daffy 19.

Lefty Grove warms up before a game. Starting in 1929 he led the Philadelphia Athletics to three straight pennants. Grove's .680 winning percentage (300-141) is the best of any 300-game winner.

of sport. The Red Sox, having emulated biblical Esau, have never won a World Series since.

Ruth had been an ace pitcher but was such a strong hitter that in 1918 he also began playing right field so he could be in the lineup more often. The Yankees made him a full-time outfielder, and he responded by belting an astounding 54 home runs. The turnstiles hummed. Everyone wanted to see the 6-foot-2-inch moon-faced slugger with the spindly legs, not just for his big swing and long drives but also for his larger-than-life personality. The Babe was a good-natured barbarian with gargantuan appetites. Former Boston teammate Harry Hooper remembered that he would "order half a dozen hot dogs and as many bottles of soda pop, stuff them in, one after another, give a few big belches, and then roar, 'OK, boys, let's go.'" He played many a game with a monumental hangover—in those Prohibition days—and was a big-league womanizer, too, though such things were kept quiet in that era.

A livelier and cleaner ball and the outlawing of trick pitches helped Ruth and other hitters. Games became slugfests, .400 averages far from rare. Between 1920 and '24 the St. Louis Cardinals' Rogers Hornsby hit .400 three times. In 1922, across town, George Sisler proved that even the dismal Browns could have a star. Sisler banged a record 257 hits and batted .420.

In June 1925 Yankee first baseman Wally Pipp sat out a game with a headache and was subbed for by 21-year-old Lou Gehrig *(opposite)*. Pipp never got back into the lineup. "I took the two most expensive aspirins in history," he said. Gehrig teamed with Ruth to form baseball's greatest one-two punch. In 1927, when Ruth hit his historic 60 homers, Gehrig slugged 47 for a Yankee club often called the best ever assembled.

Although he always played in Ruth's shadow, Gehrig holds the major-league career record for grand slam home runs with 23, and the American League record for RBIs in a season with 184. He also hit four home runs in a game—a feat the Babe never accomplished.

Gehrig set another record that seemed unbreakable: From the day he replaced Wally Pipp he never missed a game, playing 2,130 in a row over the next 14 years and earning the nickname the Iron Horse. But in 1938 teammates began to notice that he wasn't playing with his usual power, and early the next season he took himself out of the lineup, weakened by a rare and incurable illness called amyotrophic lateral sclerosis (soon to become known as Lou Gehrig's disease). The team held a farewell day for him a few months later, which itself set a big-league record for poignancy. He died in 1941.

The Depression Era. In 1930, the first season after the Wall Street crash, attendance was falling, and National League owners juiced up the baseball in an effort to boost ticket sales. The result was what Ring Lardner called "B'rer Rabbit Ball." The entire league batted a robust .303, with four members of the last-place Philadelphia Phillies exceeding .340. A year later, when the ball was deadened to restore a balance between hitting and pitching, batting averages fell by 50 points.

Some sluggers prospered anyway. The Giants' stocky, 5-foot-9-inch Mel Ott took advantage of the ludicrously short foul lines in New York's Polo Grounds to hit 29 homers that year and a total of 511 in his 22-year career. Hank Greenberg of the Detroit Tigers clouted 58 homers—just two short of the Babe's record—in 1938 and batted .326 for the decade.

The period also featured great pitching. In 1930 and '31 Lefty Grove of the Philadelphia Athletics *(opposite, bottom)* was nearly unbeatable, going 28-5 and 31-4. One sportswriter said Grove was so quick he could "throw a lamb chop past a wolf." His National League counterpart was Carl Hubbell—"the Meal Ticket"—who won 253 games for the Giants between 1928 and 1943. Hubbell threw so many "screwballs" that his left palm turned outward permanently. In 1932 the St. Louis Cardinals signed one Jay Hanna "Dizzy" Dean *(opposite, top)*, an Arkansas country boy with a broad grin. In his first five seasons Dean averaged 24 wins and pronounced himself "the greatest pitcher in the world," adding, "It ain't braggin' if you go out and do it."

Despite the stars' heroics, the Depression cut deeply into gate receipts. To boost interest, *Chicago Tribune* sports

A dying Lou Gehrig (shown in his prime in the inset) wipes away a tear during his farewell address on July 4, 1939. The memory of his brave words (below) echoing around Yankee Stadium lives on.

> "Fans, for the past two weeks you have been reading about a bad break I got. Yet today, I consider myself the luckiest man on the face of the earth."

Lou Gehrig

editor Arch Ward talked the owners into holding a mid-season All-Star Game for which the fans would pick the starting lineups. The first contest took place at Chicago's Comiskey Park on July 6, 1933. Sparked by Ruth's two-run homer, the American League won, 4-2. Play-by-play radio broadcasts also became common during the decade, and in St. Louis, Branch Rickey, general manager of the Cardinals, set up the first "farm" system—a network of small-town minor-league teams on which young players could gain training and experience. Late in the decade came the most astonishing pitching feat of that or any era: In 1938 Cincinnati southpaw Johnny Vander Meer fired back-to-back no-hitters against Boston and Brooklyn.

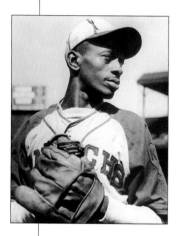

The Negro Leagues. The best pitcher in baseball during those years may not even have been in the major leagues. Tall and gangly Leroy "Satchel" Paige *(inset)* owned a wicked fastball and a bag of trick pitches that could baffle big-league hitters. Paige, however, faced them only in exhibition games because he was black, and the majors were unassailably lily-white.

African Americans nevertheless excelled at the game. Early in the century pitcher Andrew "Rube" Foster, shortstop John Henry "Pop" Lloyd, and other blacks impressed all but the most willfully blind whites. Blacks played in their own pro leagues, separate and manifestly unequal. The Negro National League began in 1920, and over the next 40 years four circuits operated at one time or another, their teams barnstorming across the United States and visiting Cuba and Central America.

The superb skills of players like Josh Gibson became known even in the white world. Although black baseball kept no official statistics, Gibson hit an estimated 70 home runs a year over a 15-year career. Writers called him the black Babe Ruth; Gibson's fans argued that Ruth should be called the white Josh Gibson.

Negro League All-Stars at the 1939 game in Chicago's Comiskey Park included two future Hall of Famers—first baseman Buck Leonard (standing, far left) and catcher Josh Gibson (standing, third from right) of the Homestead Grays. African American fans chose the teams by voting on ballots printed in the black weekly newspapers the Chicago Defender and the Pittsburgh Courier. The colorful pennants at right are from three of the league's top franchises.

Excited boys watch as Yankee center fielder Joe DiMaggio signs autographs before an exhibition game in April 1940.

Black baseball sometimes set the off-field pace, too. As early as 1929 the Kansas City Monarchs began toting around floodlights and a generator so they could play at night. The major leagues didn't have night baseball until 1935.

A New Generation of Stars. As important as the innovations of the 1930s was the arrival late in the decade of three rookies destined for greatness: Joe DiMaggio *(left and below)*, Ted Williams, and Bob Feller. The addition of DiMaggio to the Yankees initiated a new era of Yankee supremacy; in his seven seasons before joining the army, New York won six pennants and five World Series. He was a peerless center fielder who hit with both consistency and power. His record 56-game hitting streak electrified the nation in 1941 *(right)*. More than that, "DiMag" epitomized grace on the field and dignity both on and off it. No other outfielder ever moved more surely and smoothly toward a fly ball, and his long-striding swing is etched in the memory of anyone who saw it.

Despite his streak, DiMaggio did not monopolize batting honors in 1941. That same year Ted Williams of the Red Sox *(page 48)*, in just his third season in the bigs, hit .406. No one has reached the magic .400 mark since. The lanky Williams may well have been the finest natural hitter of all time, a man with eyesight so keen that it was claimed he could see the seams on a pitched ball. A cocky rookie, Williams grew into a surly, bullheaded star who feuded continually with Boston reporters and fans.

Bob Feller became a Cleveland Indian at 17, straight off an Iowa farm and already throwing the fastest pitches anybody had ever seen. Between 1938 and 1941, pitching with a leg kick that seemed to reach the sky, Feller won 93 games, threw an unprecedented opening day no-hitter, and struck out a record-breaking 18 men in a game.

DiMaggio, Williams, and Feller were just three of about 340 big-league ballplayers and 3,000 minor-leaguers who laid aside the game to serve in the armed forces in World War II. To help maintain public morale, President Roosevelt urged major-league ball to keep going, though teams' rosters were largely depleted of

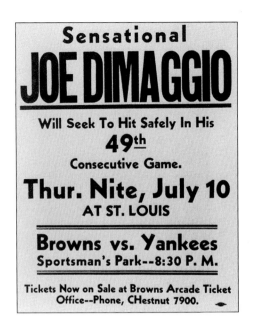

Sensational
JOE DIMAGGIO
Will Seek To Hit Safely In His
49th
Consecutive Game.
Thur. Nite, July 10
AT ST. LOUIS
Browns vs. Yankees
Sportsman's Park--8:30 P.M.

Tickets Now on Sale at Browns Arcade Ticket Office--Phone, CHestnut 7900.

His classic follow-through on full display, DiMaggio lashes a base hit during his 56-game hitting streak in 1941. He broke the record of 44 set by Willie Keeler of the old Baltimore Orioles in 1897. DiMaggio's streak began against the White Sox on May 15 and ended in Cleveland on July 17. He then hit safely in the next 16 games. When the Yanks came to town, home teams plugged the streak to boost attendance (above).

The Kenosha (Wisconsin) Comets (above) were one of four charter teams in the All-American Girls Professional Baseball League, which opened in 1943 to add diversion and pleasure to the tense lives of Americans on the home front during World War II. The women were paid $50 to $85 a week, depending on ability. At right Dorothy Harrell of the Chicago Colleens goes high to spear a line drive. At first more like softball than baseball, the women's game evolved until,

by 1948, it had essentially the same specifications as major-league ball. At its peak in 1948 the league had 10 teams.

talent. Some minor leagues suspended play for the duration. Matching opportunity with need, Cubs owner Philip K. Wrigley responded to the situation by launching the All-American Girls Professional Baseball League *(left)*, which began with four teams. The league offered crisp, entertaining play and by 1946 had won enough adherents to draw an attendance of nearly one million. But once the men returned, the women's game was fighting a losing battle; the league finally folded in 1954.

Changing the Game Forever. When John Roosevelt "Jackie" Robinson *(right)* slid home for the first time in a big-league game in the spring of 1947, he carried with him a huge load of history and emotion. In April, as a new Brooklyn Dodger, he became the first African American ever to be allowed in "the American game"—one of the most momentous events in all of American sport. It happened because of two extraordinary men: Dodger executive Branch Rickey, who felt the time was right to crack baseball's unofficial but iron-hard color line, and Robinson himself, who fit Rickey's prescription for the kind of player the task required—intelligent, dignified, highly talented, and above all cool-headed.

An all-around athlete at UCLA, infielder Robinson had proved his talent during a year with the Dodgers' minor-league team in Montreal, during which he also got a preview of the ugliness to come. Moving up to Brooklyn, Robinson became a star, hitting .297 and winning the first Rookie of the Year award in 1947 as the Dodgers took the pennant. From the outset he endured anonymous death threats and a torrent of obscenely racist abuse from opponents and spectators. Even some of his own teammates threatened to go on strike if he played. He never retaliated. His primary champion on the team was shortstop Pee Wee Reese, who said flatly, "If [Robinson] can take my job, he's entitled to it." Gradually, Robinson's talent and verve muffled the racists. A good fielder and heady hitter, he rivaled Ty Cobb as a base runner. The sight of Robinson dancing off third base, darting halfway down the line, unsettled many a pitcher. Black talent flowed into the major leagues in Robinson's wake. The Indians signed Larry Doby and Satchel Paige, who, though 42 years old by then, helped Cleveland win the 1948

Stealing home in 1949, Jackie Robinson displays the aggressive base running style he brought from the Negro National League. Robinson wrote: "The Dodgers were a championship team because all of us had learned something. I had learned how to answer insults, violence, and injustice with silence. My teammates had learned that it's not skin color but talent and ability that counts."

pennant; the Giants, Monte Irvin; the Dodgers, Roy Campanella. All of them, and Robinson, were later enshrined in the Hall of Fame.

The New York Monopoly. From 1949 to 1956 either the Dodgers or the Giants won every National League pennant but one. With the Yankees still dominating the American League, baseball became, in the words of writer Roger Angell, "almost a private possession of New York City."

New Yorkers argued endlessly about their favorite players. Who was the best center fielder? Switch-hitting Mickey Mantle, who batted .353 with 52 home runs and 130 RBIs for the Yankees in 1956? The Giants' all-round superstar Willie Mays, who had 51 homers, 127 RBIs, and an average of .319 in 1955? Or the Dodgers' Duke Snider, with 42 homers, 136 runs knocked in, and a .309 batting average the same year? And who was the better catcher?

Casey Stengel

Three-time National League MVP Campanella of the Dodgers or three-time American League MVP Yogi Berra of the Yankees?

The mastermind behind the Yankees was manager Casey Stengel *(inset)*. With a mediocre managerial record before reaching the Yanks, Stengel seemed an odd choice for the plum of major-league managing jobs. He inherited a team with great pitching and plenty of other talent—as well as a penchant for high living on the part of bosom-buddy stars Mantle, second baseman Billy Martin, and pitcher Whitey Ford. Stengel manipulated his players like chessmen, "platooning" them to get lefty-righty match-ups and relying on relief pitchers to close out victories. Between 1949 and 1960 his Yankees won 10 pennants and seven World Series; five of the Series were with the Dodgers, one with the Giants. But Stengel was best known for his gift of gab and puzzling locutions. He once said, for example, "Good pitching will always stop good hitting, and vice versa," and "I'll never make the mistake of being 70 again."

New York baseball in this era accounted for some of the game's most unforgettable moments. In 1951 the Giants trailed the first-place Dodgers by 13½ games in mid-August but finished the season with a sensational 37-7 run to tie Brooklyn on the final day. The teams split the first two games of a three-game play-off. With the Giants trailing 4-2 in the ninth inning of game 3, Bobby Thomson strode to the plate with one out to face Dodgers relief ace Ralph Branca. Thomson had homered off Branca to win game 1.

New York City's Heroes

Players who helped the Yankees, Dodgers, and Giants win 14 pennants and all eight World Series between 1949 and 1956 ranged from superstar Willie Mays to journeyman Dusty Rhodes.

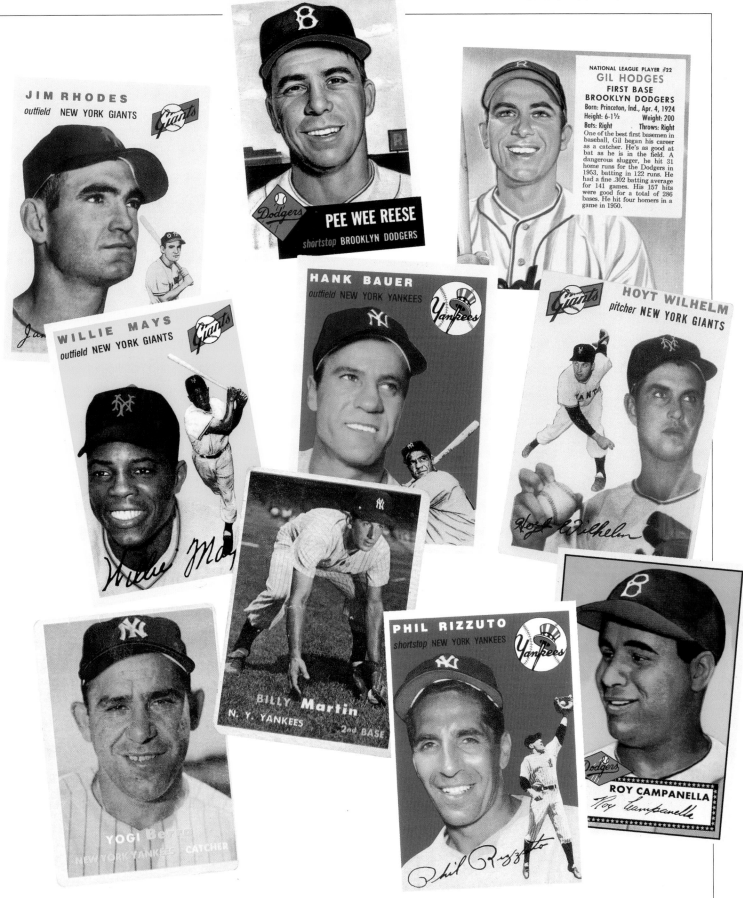

Willie Mays catches up to a tremendous drive off the bat of Cleveland's Vic Wertz at the cavernous Polo Grounds to save game 1 of the 1954 World Series. Though a highlight of baseball history, the catch, according to Mays, was not the best he ever made.

Now, with the season on the line, he stroked Branca's second pitch deep to left, where it cleared the wall by the smallest of margins, capping a miraculous Giants stretch drive as the Polo Grounds crowd and his teammates went wild. Thomson's blow was dubbed "the shot heard round the world," which was only a slight exaggeration. Radio listeners around the country heard hysterical Giants announcer Russ Hodges scream, "The Giants win the pennant! The Giants win the pennant!" over and over again.

In 1954 the Giants came to the World Series as a big underdog to the mighty Cleveland Indians, who had won an American League record 111 games during the regular season. Game 1 was tied 2-2 in the eighth when Indians first baseman Vic Wertz came to bat with runners on first and second and nobody out. He simply creamed the first pitch, driving a fly ball to deepest center field of the bathtub-shaped Polo Grounds. The Giants' Willie Mays took off running and made a sensational over-the-shoulder catch about 450 feet away *(left),* then held the lead runner at third with a prodigious throw. In the bottom of the 10th, Giants pinch hitter Dusty Rhodes hit a pop-up that was tracked by the Indians' second baseman—till it drifted over the absurdly close-in right field fence for a game-winning home run. The demoralized Tribe never recovered and was swept, 4 games to 0.

In 1955 it was the turn of the Dodgers, also lovingly known as Dem Bums. Their fans' perennial wail of "Wait till next year" was forgotten, as they finally overcame the hated Yankees for their first World Series triumph ever —touching off wild jubilation in the streets of Brooklyn. It was also the first win in Series history by a team that had trailed two games to none. Ironically, a year later the Yankees became the second team to accomplish that feat, losing the first two games and then coming back to beat . . . the Dodgers. One of the Yankee wins was the only perfect game—27 up, 27 down—ever pitched in a World Series, by an otherwise undistinguished hurler named Don Larsen.

Then, suddenly, New York City's endless champagne stopped flowing. Dodger owner Walter O'Malley, not content with the full houses he was drawing at little Ebbets Field, threatened to move unless city officials built him a new stadium. They refused, and in 1958 O'Malley whisked the Dodgers off to the rich virgin territory of Los Angeles, breaking Brooklyn's heart in the process.

Other teams had already relocated—the Braves from Boston to Milwaukee, the hapless Browns from St. Louis to Baltimore—and the Washington Senators would soon head for Minneapolis. But the Dodgers leaving Brooklyn and

Mays's glove

47

their faithful, sometimes crazy, fans? Unthinkable, but it happened. And to maintain the Dodgers-Giants rivalry, O'Malley persuaded Giants owner Horace Stoneham to move his club to San Francisco.

The Dodgers had been in Brooklyn since 1890, the Giants in upper Manhattan since 1883. In the wink of an eye New York went from a three-team to a one-team town. When two New York writers each named the three worst human beings of all time, their lists read: Hitler, Stalin, and Walter O'Malley.

Contrary to the New York writers' beliefs, great baseball—and great players—also existed outside Gotham in the '50s. The National League's chief ornaments were a hitter and a pitcher —Stan "the Man" Musial *(inset)* and Warren Spahn. Filling ballparks all around the American League was the incomparable Ted Williams *(left)*.

Musial became a Cardinals regular in 1943, batting .357 to win the first of his seven National League titles. He had a strange, corkscrew stance that one pitcher described as looking like "a kid peeking around a corner to see if the cops are coming." But his swing was a thing of beauty— like "cracking a bullwhip," one scout said. At age 41, a grandfather, he batted .330. He retired in 1963 with 3,630 hits, including 475 home runs.

Williams, after missing three full seasons while serving as a marine fighter pilot during World War II, picked up in 1946 where he left off, tearing the cover off the ball at a .342 clip as the Red Sox made it to the World Series for the only time in his career (and lost to the Cardinals 4-3). To the dismay of Boston fans, Williams was recalled to combat in the Korean War, missing two more seasons. Even so, he

Ted Williams talks about his favorite subject—hitting—for a rapt audience of fans and players before a 1957 spring training game. That year, at age 39, Williams hit .388 with 38 home runs.

> "I commenced winning pennants when I came here but I didn't commence getting any younger."
>
> Casey Stengel, upon being fired by the Yankees after the 1960 World Series

Batting left-handed, Mickey Mantle displays the powerful swing that produced a record 18 World Series home runs. In 1953, batting right-handed, he hit a 565-foot bomb out of Washington's Griffith Stadium, inspiring the term "tape measure home run." Mantle said he never swung at a ball he "didn't try to hit out of the park."

ended up with 521 home runs, retiring in 1960 after batting .316 at age 42. He departed in dramatic fashion—by hitting a home run in his very last turn at the plate.

Among pitchers, the Braves' Warren Spahn was the equal of DiMaggio and Williams. Not in image—he was consistently underhyped—but in ability. Still throwing strikes at 44, he racked up 363 victories, more than any left-hander in baseball history. In the Braves' pennant-winning season of 1948, when they rode on the strong arms of Spahn and Johnny Sain—and little else—Boston fans uttered a prayer for "Spahn and Sain and two days of rain." Unlike his crosstown colleague Williams, when the Braves moved to Milwaukee he got two more chances at the World Series, helping his team beat the Yankees in '57. The one achievement that eluded Spahn was a no-hitter—until he threw one against the Phillies when he was 39 years old. For good measure, he tossed another one at the Giants when he was 40.

The Roller Coaster '60s. The Yankees were overwhelming favorites going into the 1960 World Series against the Pittsburgh Pirates. True to form, they racked up a spectacular team batting average of .338 and outscored the Pirates by a walloping 38-3 in the three games they won. But it takes four to win the Series, and somehow the Pirates managed to win three of their own—by scores of 6-4, 3-2, and 5-2—before taking the clincher 10-9 on Bill Mazeroski's ninth-inning home run.

Bouncing back the following year, the Bronx Bombers used a Series win over Cincinnati to cap one of the most extraordinary seasons in American League history. The league gained two "expansion" teams in 1961, the Los Angeles (later California, then Anaheim) Angels and a new Washington Senators franchise. With expansion came a season lengthened to 162 games, as well as the most serious assault on Babe Ruth's single-season home-run record since Hank Greenberg's run at it in 1938. The Yankees' "M&M boys," Mickey Mantle *(left)* and Roger Maris *(right),* began hitting the ball out of the park at a Ruthian clip.

If anyone was going to break the 60-homer record, the fans wanted it to be Mantle—the successor to DiMaggio, the superstar, the longtime favorite. But in the great home-run race of '61, Mantle stalled at 54. His roommate, Maris, a shy, sensitive man who had hit only 97 homers in his whole career going into that season, hit 61. He got the record breaker on closing day,

Roger Maris blasts one of
his 61 home runs in 1961.
He felt so much pressure
during his pursuit of Babe
Ruth's hallowed record that
his hair began to fall out.

Los Angeles's awesome Sandy Koufax went 111-34 between 1962 and '66. Arthritis in his left arm ended his career at age 30.

A jubilant Denny McClain (right) is hugged by Al Kaline after winning his 30th game in 1968. He finished 31-6 with an ERA of 1.96.

though Commissioner Ford Frick had it put in the books with an asterisk denoting the longer season.

The following year a record 3,001 homers were hit in the majors. Concerned that expansion had dangerously diluted pitching quality, Commissioner Frick got the Rules Committee to expand the strike zone—making it from the top of the shoulders to the bottom of the knees, its original size before a 1950 change that placed it between the armpits and the top of the knees. (In later years the strike zone would periodically expand and contract, often seemingly at the whim of individual umpires.)

The change had no discernible effect on the game's top hitters. The Pittsburgh Pirates' great right fielder, Roberto Clemente hit well over .300 nine times during the decade. Brooks Robinson sparkled for the Orioles, joined by slugger Frank Robinson in 1966 *(page 54)*.

Even so, a host of talented pitchers dominated the game in the 1960s to an extent not seen since the dead-ball days. As historian Geoffrey C. Ward has noted, "Nineteen sixty-eight became the best year for pitchers in baseball history." That season Red Sox star Carl Yastrzemski *(page 54)* led the American League in hitting with a paltry .301, two points less than the entire National League hit in 1930, and 20 percent of the games were shutouts.

Setting that standard were such intimidating hurlers as Don Drysdale, who in 1968 recorded six shutouts in succession for the Dodgers; Juan Marichal of the Giants, one of the best of the ever growing number of Latin American players; Jim Palmer, who won three Cy Young awards with the dominant Orioles; the Mets' Tom Seaver *(page 54),* who was so much in the mythic Hardy Boys mold that he earned the nickname Tom Terrific; the Tigers' trouble-prone Denny McClain *(left),* who became the first pitcher in a third of a century to top 30 victories in a season; and especially Bob Gibson of the Cardinals *(right)* and Sandy Koufax of the Dodgers *(left, top).*

During their prime, Gibson and Koufax were as close to invulnerable as pitchers can be. In 1968 the fiercely competitive Gibson notched 22 wins (13 of them shutouts), 17 strikeouts in one World Series game, and the lowest National League earned-run average (1.12) in 62 years. Koufax was just as intimidating. Although he declined to throw at hitters, he once called his craft "the art of instilling fear by making a man flinch." He did that with as effective a fastball/curve ball combination as the game has seen. Among his achievements: four no-hitters and three Cy Young awards—when that honor covered *both* leagues. He also showed himself a man of principle, refusing to pitch a World Series game that fell on Yom Kippur, the holiest day on the calendar of his religion, Judaism.

Hard-nosed Bob Gibson of St. Louis pitched three complete-game victories over the Red Sox in the 1967 World Series, yielding a total of just 14 hits.

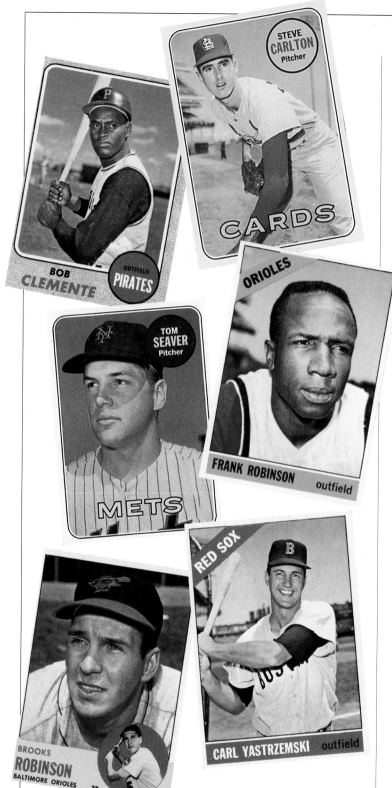

These Hall of Famers dominated base-ball in the late 1960s and 1970s. In 1974 Frank Robinson became the big leagues' first black manager. Puerto Rican star Roberto Clemente hit .414 and was named MVP of the 1971 World Series. In 1972 he died in a plane crash carrying aid to earthquake-stricken Nicaragua.

Home-run duels and masterful pitching were all very well, but the most entertaining story of the decade was unquestionably the saga of the New York Mets. Five days after the Yankees lost the '60 World Series to the underdog Pirates, Yankee top brass, in a breathtaking display of ingratitude, pushed Casey Stengel out the door. But the "Ol' Perfesser's" 50 years of baseball knowledge did not go to waste. In 1962 he was named manager of the Mets, one of two teams—the other was the Houston Colt .45s, later the renamed Astros—that the National League added the year after the American League expansion. The Mets were, as Stengel described them, "amazin' "—mostly for their hilariously inept play. The roster was stocked mostly with retreads, who lost a near-record 120 games in their first year and prompted Stengel to utter a classic lament, "Can't anyone here play this game?"

Just as amazing, Roger Angell wrote, was that "New York took this losing team to its bosom. . . . There's more Met than Yankee in all of us." Nearly as astounding was the team's 1969 achievement: After a ninth-place finish in '68, the Mets won the pennant—and then the World Series.

The Emancipation of Ballplayers. Since the beginnings of baseball the so-called reserve clause had legally bound players to their club and its wishes. Now came Cardinals outfielder Curt Flood, a sensitive and—it turned out—highly principled man. Traded in 1969 to the lowly Phillies, Flood refused to report the following spring, saying, "After 12 years in the Major Leagues, I do not feel that I am a piece of property." He demanded that all clubs be allowed to bid for his services.

Team owners warned of disaster if the courageous Flood's position prevailed. But prevail it did, through a series of 1970s legal challenges by Flood and a few other players. The reserve clause was overturned, with astonishing results: In the late 1950s most players earned less than $25,000, and even the Mayses and Mantles made little over $100,000. By the mid-'80s the average player salary was $371,000, and 30 stars were making more than $1 million. At century's end, the *average* salary topped $1.7 million.

Other important changes came voluntarily. With four

Henry Aaron watches homer
number 715 leave Atlanta's
Fulton County Stadium to break
Babe Ruth's lifetime home-run
mark. By the time he retired
in 1976 after a 23-year career,
"Hammerin' Hank" had exceeded
the Babe's old record by 40.

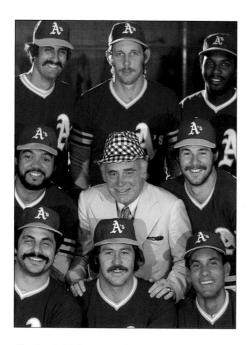

Charles O. Finley, eccentric owner of the Oakland Athletics, is surrounded by some of the players who led the team to three straight World Series titles— the only team other than the Yankees to accomplish that feat—between 1972 and 1974. Sporting the fashionable facial hair of the period and wearing the garish green-and-yellow uniforms dreamed up by Finley are (clockwise from upper left) relief pitcher Rollie Fingers, outfielder Joe Rudi, pitcher Vida Blue, catcher Gene Tenace, shortstop Bert Campaneris, pitcher Jim "Catfish" Hunter, third baseman Sal Bando, and outfielder Reggie Jackson.

"We have a nucleus of guys who give 100% 100% of the time. [They] are not just satisfied with … a big salary. … They want to win."

A's third baseman Sal Bando

new teams in each league, the leagues were split into two divisions each in 1969, with play-off series to determine pennant winners. In 1973 the American League adopted a rule allowing a "designated hitter" to bat for the pitcher. Both changes infuriated purists.

While baseball was accommodating itself to these changes, three players —a great slugger, a compiler of massive hit totals, and a new Iron Man— used amazingly long careers to rewrite the record books. When Henry Aaron *(page 55)* hit his first home run for the Milwaukee Braves in 1954, no one imagined that the wiry outfielder would one day break Babe Ruth's career home-run mark of 714. Aaron could do it all—catch, throw, run, and, above all, hit for power. Unfortunately, his march toward the Babe's record provoked a reappearance of racist ugliness such as had not been seen since Jackie Robinson's rookie year. Aaron socked the magical home run number 715 on April 8, 1974, despite being deluged with hate mail and receiving death threats.

Reds infielder Pete Rose *(far right, bottom)* regularly banged out 200-plus hits a year. In his rookie season other players derisively called him Charlie Hustle because he ran to first base on walks. Yet the nickname became a badge of honor for his old-school style of play, typified in the 1970 All-Star Game, which he won by barreling into catcher Ray Fosse and breaking Fosse's collarbone while jarring the ball loose. Said Rose, unrepentant: "I could never have looked my father in the eye if I hadn't hit Fosse."

With catcher Johnny Bench *(near right)* and second baseman Joe Morgan *(far right, top)*, Rose formed the heart of one of baseball's greatest teams. Winning the National League pennant but losing the World Series in 1970 and '72, the Big Red Machine, as that Cincinnati team came to be called, beat the Red Sox in the Series in 1975 and swept the Yankees in '76 for manager Sparky Anderson.

In 1978 Rose hit safely in 44 straight games to set the modern National League record. But the following year he became a free agent and signed with the Phillies for a million dollars. In 1980 he helped his new team to its first World Series championship. Rose returned to the Reds in 1984 and capped his 24-year career by surpassing Ty Cobb's lifetime hit total, finishing with 4,256.

To counter the Big Red Machine, the American League had a machine of its own—a green, gold, and white one. The Oakland Athletics, a feisty bunch who often battled one another as much as they did opponents, were assembled by owner Charles Finley *(above, left)*, an equally feisty ex-insurance salesman who had so worn out his welcome by the time the A's deserted Kansas City for Oakland in 1968 that Missouri senator Stuart Symington declared their new home "the luckiest city since Hiroshima." Finley made

Joe Morgan singles in the winning run for the Reds in game 7 of the 1975 Series. He is the only second baseman to win back-to-back Most Valuable Player awards.

Johnny Bench of Cincinnati's "Big Red Machine" tracks a pop foul. Bench topped 20 homers 11 times and drove in more than 100 runs six times. He caught 100 games or more for 13 straight years and played the entire 1975 season without a passed ball.

Pete Rose, shown launching a head-first slide, led Cincinnati in all-out effort. "I've got to give 110 percent," he said. "The minute I slack off, I've had it."

his team a modish representation of 1970s fashions. To go with their out-landishly colored new uniforms he offered the players a $300 bonus to grow long hair and beards or mustaches.

The A's may have looked strange and may have set a major-league record for team dissension, but they achieved something even the Reds could not: three World Series titles in a row. The A's won largely with the slugging of Reggie Jackson, tight infield play, and the pitching of "Catfish" Hunter, Vida Blue, and reliever Rollie Fingers.

With all their success, however, many of the A's stars were unhappy un-der Finley's interfering ownership, and soon both Catfish Hunter and Reggie Jackson *(left)* were climbing into Yankee pinstripes. They were among the fruits of a free-spending campaign by the Yankees' new principal owner, the imperious George Steinbrenner, who had purchased the club from CBS in 1973. Steinbrenner spent so much on free-agent players that wags called the Yankees "the best team money can buy." He signed Hunter for a then-record $3.75 million over three years. Baseball had entered an era in which the depth of a franchise's pockets counted for more than maintaining a good farm system.

For the Yankees, Jackson became "Mr. October," the man who delivered bundles of home runs in World Series games. His greatest performance came in game 6 of the 1977 Series against the Dodgers: three home runs—a Series record—in three consecutive times at bat off three different pitchers.

The Root of Baseball Evil. October heroics couldn't insulate the game against its internal problems. Among those were player-owner disputes over money and an alarming increase in substance abuse among players. Three months into the 1981 season, the players went on strike over an attempt by owners to undercut free agency by insisting that, for every free agent they lost, they be reimbursed with cash or a player of comparable ability. Base-ball officials, scrambling to impose some order on the season after the seven-week walkout, split it in two, with the division "winners" of the first half of the 111-game season to vie with the second-half leaders in pennant play-offs.

The owners tried to retaliate in 1985. Three of the game's best players —White Sox catcher Carlton Fisk, outfielder Andre Dawson of the Montreal Expos, and pitcher Jack Morris of the Tigers—became free agents. Yet other

At right, from top to bottom, Mike Schmidt, Nolan Ryan, and Rickey Henderson personified power hitting, power pitching, and power base running, respectively, in the 1980s. Schmidt hit 548 home runs and had 1,595 RBIs; Ryan struck out a record 5,714 and threw seven no-hitters; Henderson stole a record 130 bases in one season.

Boggs and Gwynn won a combined 13 batting titles; Maddux and Clemens, nine Cy Youngs. Puckett led the Twins to two World Series titles.

teams declined to sign them. Marvin Miller, executive director of the Players Association, smelled a rat. He charged that all 26 clubs and the commissioner had conspired to freeze out the three. Arbitrators agreed; the owners were found guilty of collusion and ordered to pay $280 million in lost wages.

Fans, tired of this new primacy of money over sport, were uncertain whether to support the high-salaried players or the multimillionaire owners. The public became further disillusioned when a drug scandal broke. More than 50 players admitted that they had used cocaine, and the Mets' Keith Hernandez estimated that 40 percent of big-league players had sampled it. Mets pitcher Dwight Gooden—fresh off a season in which he won 24 games—entered a drug abuse treatment program. Reliever Steve Howe was suspended *seven* times for substance abuse between 1983 and 1991, but each time baseball's brass allowed him to return.

But always, the game rose above the off-the-field ugliness to rivet fan attention with its drama of glorious success and heartbreaking failure. In 1986 the Red Sox were one out away from winning their first World Series since 1918. They led the Mets three games to two and were ahead 5-3 in the bottom of the 10th inning of game 6 with two out and nobody on base. It was almost time to start popping champagne corks.

Boston fans believe the Red Sox have been cursed since the sale of Babe Ruth, and what happened next did nothing to dispel that notion. The Mets got three singles in a row, and a run scored. In came a new Boston pitcher, who promptly uncorked a wild pitch—game tied. Then Mookie Wilson hit a routine roller toward first base. The ball went right through the legs of ailing Boston first baseman Bill Buckner—Mets win. Game 7 the next night surprised no one: Mets 8, Red Sox 5.

Baseball suffered another black eye in 1989 when Pete Rose, Charlie Hustle himself, was permanently banned from the game by Commissioner Bart Giamatti for allegedly betting on games—including some involving his own Cincinnati Reds. Despite having stroked more hits than anyone else who ever played the game, Pete Rose was shut out of the Baseball Hall of Fame.

In the 1990s, player-management relations frayed again. When the owners insisted on firm salary caps, the players in 1994 staged a late-season strike that resulted in the unthinkable—the cancellation of the remainder of the season, the play-offs, and the World Series.

Baltimore Iron Man Cal Ripken deftly scoops up a grounder and flips to first— a play he made for 2,632 consecutive games in breaking Lou Gehrig's record. The streak ended on September 20, 1998, when Ripken voluntarily sat out a game.

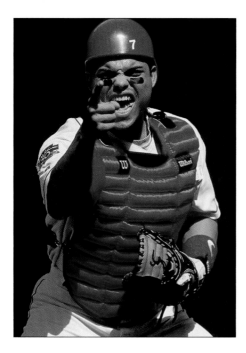

Rifle-armed catcher Ivan Rodriguez of the Texas Rangers threw out 52.5 percent of would-be base stealers in 1998, the best mark recorded since the statistic was first kept in 1989.

Randy Johnson delivers heat. The 6-foot-10-inch southpaw began the 1999 season with a career average of 10.6 strikeouts per nine innings—the best in big-league history.

Then another hero emerged. Just as Babe Ruth's home runs had brought baseball back from the depths of the Black Sox scandal, the consecutive-game streak of the Orioles' Cal Ripken Jr. *(page 61)* captivated the nation. During 14 years as the Orioles' star shortstop, Ripken had relentlessly chipped away at Lou Gehrig's mark of 2,130 games in a row. The streak reached a glorious climax late in the 1995 season. On September 5, before a sellout crowd at Baltimore's Camden Yards and a national television audience, he tied Gehrig's mark and slammed a home run.

The next night, when he broke the record, Ripken was hailed by President Bill Clinton and a rosterful of baseball immortals. A sign at the ballpark read: "Cal, Thank You For Saving Baseball." After completing the top of the fifth inning to make number 2,131 official, Ripken took a victory lap around the field, shaking hands with fans and players alike. Veteran umpire Al Clark was so moved that, forgetting how Gehrig's achievement had been considered unassailable, he predicted, "This will never happen again." To put the icing on the cake, Ripken powered another homer.

Baseball at the End of the Century. The sport has overcome wars, the Great Depression, racial exclusion, desegregation, strikes, expansion, rule changes, free agency, and salary inflation. Its great performers continue to become part of American folklore. The stars of today—Ken Griffey Jr. *(right)*, Derek Jeter, Chipper Jones, Ivan "Pudge" Rodriguez *(left, top)*, Randy "the Big Unit" Johnson *(left)*, Nomar Garciaparra, and others—add each year to the vast, yeasty, infinitely rich legend of the game.

As if summoning itself to shake off troubles and demonstrate its fundamental perfection, baseball produced, in 1998, what sportswriters called "the greatest season ever." The '98 Yankees won 114 games, the most in the majors in 92 years. Managed by the universally admired Joe Torre, with antediluvian baseball man Don Zimmer at his side, they proceeded to demolish Cleveland and Texas in the play-offs and the San Diego Padres in the World Series—for a total of 125 victories and a record overall winning percentage of .704.

Lacking any superstars, the Yanks played as a smoothly interlocking unit, a genuine *team* that was far greater than the sum of its parts. Even Steinbrenner, the often malcontented owner, couldn't find anything to criticize. In the victors' World Series locker room, drenched in celebratory champagne, Steinbrenner said, "This is as good as any team that's ever played the game." For once, there was no reason to argue with him.

Beyond the Bronx, Cal Ripken extended his consecutive-game streak to 2,632 before he decided to take a day off late in the season. The Giants'

Ken Griffey Jr. is the proto-
typical 1990s superstar,
combining size, speed, and
power. He plays center field
like Willie Mays and hits
home runs like Henry Aaron.

On his way to a season record 70 home runs, Mark McGwire watches along with everyone else as number 61 sails out of Busch Stadium to tie Roger Maris's mark in September 1998.

Barry Bonds became the only player ever to hit 400 home runs and steal 400 bases. Like a younger Bonds, shortstop Alex Rodriguez of Seattle hit 42 homers and stole 46 bases. Seattle's Griffey became the youngest player ever to reach the 350-homer mark. Kerry Wood of the Cubs pitched a game in which he struck out 20, issued no walks, and gave up a single hit.

But most of all, 1998 was the year when the entire nation was enthralled by the home-run duel waged by the Cardinals' Mark McGwire *(left)* and the Cubs' Sammy Sosa *(inset)*. Like a pair of thoroughbreds, they went neck-and-neck down the stretch, giving their games, a *Sports Illustrated* writer said, "the feeling of revival meetings. . . . Baseball was a cool topic at the water cooler again. . . . McGwire or Sosa? Who do you like? How many will they hit?"

On September 8 McGwire swatted number 62 to break Maris's 37-year-old record. Sosa got his 62nd soon after, and the friendly duel remained close. Then McGwire put things out of reach by blasting five home runs with his last 19 swings of the season for a jaw-dropping total of 70. Sosa finished with 66. Their home-run balls became high-bracket collectibles, evoking stories of both selflessness and greed. One fan returned ball number 61 to McGwire for a handshake, two autographed jerseys, and two autographed bats. Another auctioned off ball number 70—and got $2.7 million from a collector.

Defying the odds, the Yankees and McGwire-Sosa (the two sluggers seemed to be joined at the hip) picked up in 1999 where they'd left off the previous year. The Yankees did not approach their '98 win total, but they again captured their division and made another Sherman-like march through the postseason, winning six of seven play-off games and a second straight World Series, over Atlanta, in a 4-0 sweep. The Bunyanesque McGwire and the compact, exuberant Sosa again made the home-run race a two-man affair and this time wound up with 65 and 63, respectively. Fans went slightly less loopy this time, and retrieved home-run balls were no longer bid up to astronomical levels. Yet the two sluggers again made the Cardinals and Cubs, noncontenders in the pennant races, big-drawing teams on the road.

Baseball in the 20th century had seen and absorbed a dizzying variety of changes. Or had it? When Don Zimmer, a 50-year veteran as a player, coach, and manager, was asked how baseball had changed during his lifetime he replied matter-of-factly: "The game is the same. Ninety feet, four balls, three strikes, three outs, 60 feet six inches. Society changes. The game's the same."

Battling the Odds

★

ATHLETES WHO REFUSED TO GIVE IN

Among the world's top athletes are a few who have displayed something beyond their sporting ability. They challenged life-threatening illnesses, battled congenital disabilities or chronic ailments, performed despite broken bones or acute sickness—and won. Thanks to unwavering vision, iron will, and inspiring courage, they transcended their extraordinary talent to beat odds even greater than those posed by the competition.

Golfer Ben Hogan was one such athlete. The 5-foot-9-inch, 160-pound son of a Texas blacksmith was reigning U.S. Open champion and the professional tour's leading money winner when, on a foggy night in February 1949, his Cadillac smashed head-on into a bus that had crossed into his lane. Lingering between life and death, Hogan lay in a hospital with a crushed pelvis and other broken bones and terrible internal injuries. Two months after the accident, when he finally graduated to a wheelchair *(inset),* he weighed 95 pounds. Doctors thought he might never walk again.

But in June of the following year the 37-year-old showed up at the U.S. Open in Merion, Pennsylvania, bandaged from hips to ankles. Grim-faced with pain and barely able to drag himself around the course, Hogan somehow stayed in contention through the first

Ben Hogan strokes one out of the rough at the 1950 U.S. Open (left). Known for a cool reserve that kept fans at a distance, he nonetheless won over the public with his comeback from a near-fatal accident.

two rounds but faced a grueling 36 holes on Saturday. During the final round his legs stiffened. "My God, I don't think I can finish," he told a friend. But the gritty Hogan did finish—and far more. He ended the round tied for first with Lloyd Mangrum and George Fazio and went on to shoot a brilliant 69 in an 18-hole play-off the next day to win. "People have always been telling me what I can't do," Hogan said. "I guess I have wanted to show them. That's been one of the driving forces all my life."

Debilitating Illness. When Wilma Rudolph was an infant her mother nursed her through one illness after another—not just the usual childhood ailments, but whooping cough, scarlet fever, and double pneumonia as well. Then, when the little girl was four, her left leg began to grow weak and twisted. Doctors said she had polio and would never walk again. But she was full of determination and belonged to a large and supportive family—18 brothers and sisters. "We didn't have too much money back then," she later said, "but we had everything else, especially love."

Every week for two years Rudolph's mother took her 50 miles to Fisk University's medical college in Nashville for therapy. Older siblings massaged her withered leg. And at nine the triumphant girl stunned doctors by removing the leg brace she had worn for years and walking unaided. "By the time I was twelve," she recalled, "I was challenging every boy in our neighborhood at running, jumping, everything."

As a teenage sprinter Rudolph attracted the notice of the track coach at Tennessee State University and attended his summer training camp. Six years later she took the 1960 Olympics in Rome by storm, winning the 100-meter and the 200-meter dashes and coming from three places back in the anchor leg of the 4 x 100-meter relay. No American woman had ever won three Olympic gold medals in track.

A generation later another young runner needed extraordinary courage when her body conspired against her. "Mentally, I was up and ready to run," said Gail Devers (*page 70*) about the 1988 Seoul Olympics. "But physically, my body was saying, 'Gail, I just can't do it.'" Devers ran poorly, failing even to qualify for the finals, and soon afterward began experiencing constant fatigue.

For the next two years she battled exhaustion, failing vision, hair loss, even a befogged mind. "It was hard for me to remember my phone number and address," she said. Doctors finally located the problem—a thyroid disorder called Graves' disease. But though no one realized it at the time, the

> "I was mad, and I was going to beat these illnesses, no matter what."
>
> Olympic champion Wilma Rudolph

Following a preliminary heat of the 200-meter dash at the 1960 Olympics in Rome, 20-year-old Wilma Rudolph exudes poised calm (above). Days later she zoomed over the finish line of the 100-meter dash (opposite) to take the first of her three gold medals. Hers had been a rough road from rural Tennessee to Olympic triumph, but her childhood resolve to overcome the crippling effects of polio paid off in glory for her and inspiration for others.

Gail Devers flies over a hurdle in the 100-meter semifinal at the 1992 Olympics. Though gold eluded her in that event, she did win the 100-meter dash—an astounding comeback for a woman who only two years before had been unable to walk. When "the walls are closing in on you," Devers said, "you've got to reach deep down inside yourself to find that inner strength."

Amy Van Dyken screams with joy, having overcome severe asthma to win the 100-meter butterfly in the 1996 Olympics. It was just one of her triumphs, as she became the first American woman to earn four gold medals in a single Olympics. "I'm really stubborn," she said. "If someone tells me I stink, I'm going to try and prove them wrong."

radiation treatments she received would turn out to be worse than the disease. Among other horrors, the skin on her feet was peeling so badly she couldn't walk. Baffled doctors were about to amputate both feet in March 1991 when they discovered that the radiation was the culprit and stopped it in favor of thyroid pills.

In a few weeks Devers managed a hobbling walk around a track; in June she won a race in New York; and in 1992 she went barreling down the track at the Barcelona Olympics to win the 100-meter dash—a victory she repeated in 1996 in Atlanta, where she also earned a gold in the 4 x 100-meter relay. Said Devers of her travail and triumph, "I don't feel that there's any hurdle too high or any obstacle in my life that I can't get over."

Equally determined was Amy Van Dyken *(bottom left)*. A severe asthmatic, Van Dyken could scarcely haul herself up a stairway as a child. To strengthen her lungs doctors introduced her to swimming when she was six. By age 12, still barely able to go the length of a pool, she was, in her own words, a "little wimpy, asthmatic weakling." But she loved swimming and found a fiercely competitive streak within herself. Despite the need for inhalers, despite the suffocating attacks and the ambulance runs to the hospital, despite the miserably low lung capacity, she struggled on, and in high school managed to get on the relay team. Still subject to terrible asthma attacks, she continued to train and improve, until at the Atlanta Olympics she capped her long struggle by taking two individual golds and two more as the anchor on winning relay teams. "When you're standing up on the medal stand and the national anthem is playing," she said, "I'd give up breathing for that."

A condition as debilitating as asthma—but more mysterious—was the burden Michelle Akers bore. Considered by some the best woman soccer player ever, Akers *(right)* waged an ongoing battle against chronic fatigue syndrome.

Michelle Akers heads the ball in the 1999 World Cup final against China. Sidelined near the end of regulation play with dehydration and a concussion, she later ripped out her IV to join the U.S. victory celebration. "Every time I look at Michelle I shake my head in disbelief," said teammate Julie Foudy. "She never, ever gives up."

His team down one point with only two seconds to go, Tom Dempsey kicks a record-breaking 63-yard field goal with his deformed foot (left). "I couldn't see where the ball came down that far away," said Dempsey. "Suddenly I saw the ref with his hands in the air and I heard the crowd, and I had to accept the fact that I'd done it."

Beset by exhaustion, vertigo, and migraines, Akers compared her condition to "the 24-hour flu—only I had it for five years." At a doctor's suggestion she changed her diet and took quarts of an electrolyte solution intravenously after play. She managed to rebuild her stamina to the point where she boosted the U.S. women's team to victory in both the 1996 Olympics and the 1999 World Cup.

Beating a Handicap. Athletes with congenital defects have to do more with less. When they rise to the challenge, the results can be deeply inspiring. Tom Dempsey *(above)* was born with a withered arm and a toeless right foot. Overcoming his fate, he learned to use the foot as a kind of mallet for kicking a football and proved good enough to make the pros. On November 8, 1970, his New Orleans Saints trailed the Detroit Lions by a point with two seconds left on the clock and were seemingly far out of kicking range. Still, the coach sent Dempsey in for a virtually impossible 63-yard field goal attempt. (The league record was 56 yards.)

"Most people had started for the parking lot," Dempsey recalled, "and some fans were laughing." The ball was snapped and placed, and Dempsey's specially shod right foot hit it dead-on. The ball seemed to float through the air in slow motion, then sailed between the uprights as the stadium erupted in wild cheering. Dempsey had raised his team to a 19-17 victory and set a pro field goal record that has never been bested.

Like Dempsey, pitcher Jim Abbott *(right)* was born with a deformed arm. Loving the game of baseball, he spent hours as a child hurling balls against a brick wall, learning to do more and more with his one hand. He developed into a talented pitcher and he perfected his "Abbott switch"—

AB　BALL　STRIKE　OUT
9　0　1　2

.318 AVG　20 HR　102 RBI
7　16　9　8　40　24　22　25　15
CF　SS　2B　LF　1B　DH　RF　3B　C
✳

The scoreboard tells the tale as one-handed pitcher Jim
Abbott of the New York Yankees gets Carlos Baerga to
make the last out of Abbott's September 1993 no-hitter
against the Cleveland Indians. The overjoyed Abbott
(inset) had left his disability behind for a spot in the
record books.

"I was bleeding internally. The doctors ordered me not to compete. But these are the Olympics and you die before you don't compete in the Olympics."

Discus champion Al Oerter

In the 1964 Olympic trials Al Oerter, wearing a brace on his neck to protect an injured disk, uncorks a 201-foot-3-inch throw. A colossus of muscle and iron will, Oerter entered four consecutive Olympics as an underdog and emerged with the gold each time.

after releasing a pitch, Abbott would whisk his glove from the stump of his right arm onto his left hand to be ready to field the ball. He led the U.S. team to victory in the 1988 Olympics and made the majors the following year. Abbott won 18 and lost 11 for the Anaheim Angels in 1991 and threw a no-hitter for the New York Yankees in 1993.

Playing Through Pain. For two straight Olympic Games, 1956 and 1960, Al Oerter had won the discus throw. But his prospects for a third consecutive gold medal seemed shattered. Two years before the 1964 Tokyo Games the muscular 260-pounder incurred a lingering injury to his neck and had to put on a neck brace *(left)*. Still, he kept training and competing, pushing himself until, with Tokyo just six days off, he tore cartilage in his rib cage.

Doctors told him he couldn't compete, but Oerter never gave their warnings a thought. Applying ice to his sides to retard internal bleeding, he made his first four throws in great pain, but he lagged in third place. "I decided the pain was too much to take a sixth throw," he said. "I would go for broke in the fifth." With a slow spin and a mighty heave, Oerter let the discus fly, then doubled over in agony. The roar of the crowd brought him snapping back up. His 200-foot-1-inch effort was two feet farther than the first-place competitor's best and set a new record. Amazingly, the indomitable Oerter wasn't ready to end his career. Fighting additional insults to his aging body, at the 1968 Olympics in Mexico City he won gold for an incredible fourth straight time.

In game 5 of the 1970 National Basketball Association (NBA) Finals between the Los Angeles Lakers and the New York Knickerbockers, Willis Reed *(number 19, right)*, captain and center for the Knicks, collapsed in pain with a deep thigh injury *(inset, right)*. Without him, the Lakers trounced the Knicks in the next game. A few days later, minutes before the final game was to begin at Madison Square Garden, no one knew if Reed would play. Then, just before the start, he limped into the arena, his thigh heavily taped. Fans jumped to their feet and burst into applause. "It's like getting your left arm sewed back on," said team-

Willis Reed vies for a rebound with Wilt Chamberlain of the Lakers in the deciding game of the 1970 NBA Finals. After collapsing with a severe thigh injury in game 5 (inset), Reed limped onto the court for game 7 and inspired his team to victory.

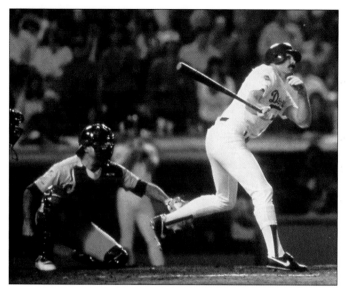

After hammering a storybook pinch-hit two-run homer (above) to win the 1988 World Series opener for the Dodgers, Kirk Gibson hobbles triumphantly around the bases (below). "Once I got up in that cage," he said later, "I didn't feel anything again until I was going around the bases."

mate Cazzie Russell. Miraculously, Reed won the tipoff against Wilt Chamberlain, then drained a shot from the top of the key, soon following it with a 20-footer. Although that was the end of Reed's scoring, the emotional boost he created helped the Knicks to a 113-99 victory and their first championship.

What Reed did for the Knicks, Kirk Gibson *(left)* did for the Los Angeles Dodgers in the 1988 World Series. In game 1 the Oakland Athletics were leading 4-3 in the bottom of the ninth. Gibson, the Dodgers' offensive spearhead, lay in the trainer's room with a torn left hamstring and an injured right knee —at least, that's where most fans thought he was. In fact, in the eighth inning Gibson had slid off the trainer's table, limped to the team's indoor batting cage, and started taking swings. After pinch hitter Mike Davis made it to first with two out, Gibson suddenly appeared, hobbling toward the plate to pinch-hit against ace reliever Dennis Eckersley. "I live for these moments," he said later.

With the count 3 and 2, Eckersley unleashed a slider that came in low over the plate, and Gibson swung. The instant the ball met the bat, Gibson knew he'd got all of it. As the ball soared toward the right-field stands, he set out on what must have been baseball's slowest victory run, gingerly placing his left leg and dragging his right to advance step by faltering step. Gibson was through for the rest of the Series, but his courage had galvanized his teammates—the Dodgers went on to vanquish the A's.

At the 1996 Atlanta Olympics, 18-year-old Kerri Strug *(right)* was considered the quiet, dependable, not-so-tough understudy on the American women's gymnastics team. But when star teammate Dominique Moceanu botched her vault landings, Strug became the Americans' last hope for victory over the Russians. On her first vault Strug sprawled on the landing. "I heard a crack in my ankle," she said, "but you hear a lot of cracks in gymnastics. Then I tried to stand up, and I realized something was really wrong. I couldn't feel my leg." With only 45 seconds to decide whether to risk a second try, she limped over to coach Bela Karolyi. "You can do it!" he whispered.

"Please, Lord, help me out here," prayed Strug, and with the world watching in silent admiration, she somehow tore down the runway toward the horse without even a limp. Springing into a clean twist at full height, she somersaulted to a sound landing and, gritting her teeth, pivoted toward the judges on one foot. With a score of 9.712, she had

Completing a winning vault despite torn ankle ligaments at the 1996 Olympics, Kerri Strug faces the judges on one foot (left, top), then collapses in pain (left, bottom). Fifteen minutes later coach Bela Karolyi carried Strug to the medal stand (above). "I didn't want to be remembered for falling on my butt in my best event," Strug said later.

Between intervals of nausea (above) and brilliant play (below), tennis champ Pete Sampras wrings victory from his opponent while wrestling with illness in a 1996 U.S. Open quarterfinal.

clinched the first team gold ever for a U.S. women's Olympic gymnastics team.

Overcoming Sickness. For tennis star Pete Sampras *(left)* 1996 was proving a terrible year. In May his beloved coach, Tim Gullikson, had died of brain cancer, and a devastated Sampras had subsequently been knocked out of the year's first three major tournaments. Now he was in the quarterfinals of the U.S. Open suffering severe heat exhaustion and dehydration. Facing Spain's Alex Corretja in the fifth-set tiebreaker of an epic four-hour-plus match, a queasy and drained Sampras reeled behind the baseline and vomited. Nearing his breaking point, he hit a serve that went long. "After that," Sampras said, "I wanted to get it over with." But his next serve zoomed in at an angle too sharp for his opponent to manage—a rare second-serve ace—and it changed everything. With Corretja serving, Sampras won the next point and the match, and the stadium erupted in deafening applause. Later, with tears in his eyes, he said, "This is for Tim. "

Nauseated, dizzy, drained—that's how the Chicago Bulls' Michael Jordan felt when he staggered onto the floor for game 5 of the 1997 NBA Finals against the Utah Jazz. "I've never seen him so sick," said teammate Scottie Pippen. "I didn't think he was going to be able to put on his uniform." Hit hard by a stomach virus, Chicago's immortal number 23 had spent the hour before the game lying in a dark room, keeping a bucket nearby in which to throw up. For most of the warmups he sat drooping on the bench.

Then the game began, and Jordan's already mind-boggling legend grew to even more incredible proportions. Awe-struck fans sat watching him hit fade-away jumpers; drive on defenders; hang suspended in midair; and, during one time-out, rest his dizzy head on a teammate's shoulder. Jordan scored the winning basket, a three-pointer, completing a stunning performance. "There's nothing more to say," said Pippen. "He's the greatest." Two nights later the Bulls wrapped up the championship.

"Doctors told me that I had bone cancer and that my leg had to be amputated. I said, 'Sure, no problem,' because I didn't know what the word amputated meant."

Diana Golden, recalling her childhood

One-legged Diana Golden proves she has the stuff to take on challenging slopes and skiers of all levels, whether disabled or not (above). Early in her career, in search of greater speed, Golden had scrapped her outrigger poles—crutches with small runners at the bottom—and replaced them with standard racing poles.

Surviving Cancer. When Diana Golden *(below, left)* was a child she was a self-proclaimed klutz. One sport—skiing—did appeal to the awkward youngster, but in 1975, when she was 12, she was diagnosed with cancer in her right leg. To save her life the leg would have to be taken off. Though devastated, Golden strapped on a single ski boot a few months later and hit the slopes. Between 1986 and 1990 she won 10 gold medals at the World Handicapped Championships, 19 U.S. titles, and a gold in the giant slalom for disabled skiers at the 1988 Calgary Olympics.

But that wasn't enough for Golden. Campaigning to change the U.S. Ski Association's practice of forcing disabled skiers to compete last, she became the driving force behind implementing the so-called Golden Rule, which put athletes with and without disabilities on more equal terms. Golden was elected the U.S. Olympic Committee's 1988 Female Skier of the Year and received the Flo Hyman Award from the Women's Sports Foundation in 1991, but possibly her most satisfying achievement as an athlete was placing 10th in a 1987 slalom, the only handicapped skier in a field of 40.

Cancer struck another athlete in the prime of his career. In 1996 25-year-old bicycle racer Lance Armstrong, ranked ninth in the world, was diagnosed with testicular cancer. Worse, the disease had already spread to his brain, abdomen, and lungs. Doctors operated and administered chemotherapy but gave him a dismal chance of survival. Though frightened for his life, Armstrong never let go of his sport. In the three-week intervals between his three debilitating chemotherapy treatments, he rode 30 to 50 miles a day to maintain some semblance of conditioning.

As time passed, miraculously Armstrong's body showed no evidence of cancer. "You spend a year so scared and terrified that you feel like you deserve the rest of your life to have a vacation," he said. "But you can't." He went back into training feeling stronger than ever and began focusing on that pinnacle of road racing, the Tour de France. Even the loss of 15 pounds during chemotherapy better prepared him for tackling the Tour's notorious mountains.

By 1999 Armstrong felt ready: "It's not just the convalescence of the body, but . . . of the spirit as well." He dominated the race from start to finish. On the final day, July 25, as he streaked down Paris's Champs-Élysées, spectators applauded his courageous victory. But Armstrong said, "I'm prouder of being a cancer survivor than I am of winning the Tour de France."

Wearing the leader's yellow jersey, Lance Armstrong wins a time trial and cements his 1999 Tour de France victory. Almost three years earlier he had been given a less than 50 percent chance of surviving his spreading cancer.

Memorable Bouts of the Century

★

GREAT CHAMPIONS, CLASSIC MATCHES

When Jack Johnson met Jim Jeffries on July 4, 1910, in Reno, Nevada, for the world heavyweight title, the fight proved an uncanny forecast of boxing in the 20th century. It featured colorful personalities, outlandish hype, controversy, and a dazzling display of punching skills.

In 1908 Johnson had become the first black heavyweight champion. A powerful 6-foot-tall 208-pounder *(inset),* he wore diamonds, flashed gold-capped teeth, and loved fast cars. He was married three times—twice to white women during an age when just looking at a white woman could get an African American lynched.

White America was in torment over Johnson, and a search was launched for a "Great White Hope" to set things aright. Finally, former champion Jeffries was lured out of a six-year retirement. "It's up to you," novelist Jack London wrote him. "The White Man must be rescued."

Promoter Tex Rickard put up a purse of $101,000. Some 20,000 spectators doubled Reno's population for the brutally hot day. Across the nation, crowds awaited telegraph reports. But the fight itself was a letdown. Jeffries was literally knocked out of the ring in the 15th round as the Reno crowd watched in stunned silence. Word of Johnson's victory sparked race riots in many American cities, and more than a dozen people were killed.

CHURCHMAN'S CIGARETTES

JACK JOHNSON

Jim Jeffries burrows in but can't dodge the blows of Jack Johnson, who had become champion by thrashing another white man, Tommy Burns. This bout was the first of many to be hyped as the "Battle of the Century."

Jack Dempsey trains in 1922. Dubbed the Manassa Mauler for his Colorado birthplace and brawling style, the popular Dempsey was a national hero during his seven-year reign as champion.

Dempsey vs. Tunney: The "Long Count" Fight

Jack Dempsey personified boxing in the 1920s the way his buddy Babe Ruth embodied baseball. Like the Babe, who could strike out in style, Dempsey cemented his status as an American icon even in defeat. Dempsey developed an aggressive fighting style early. He left home at 16 and traveled the West on freight trains, fighting in saloons for pocket change. When he officially turned pro, he intimidated opponents with an angry scowl and explosive punching.

In 1919 Dempsey fought Jess Willard for the heavyweight crown. Willard was five inches taller and 58 pounds heavier, but Dempsey knocked him down seven times in the first round and broke his nose, jaw, two ribs, and four teeth. "He was 187 pounds of unbridled violence," wrote Red Smith. Dempsey fought infrequently during the next seven years, but his bouts attracted huge crowds and generated the first million-dollar gates.

Gene Tunney made an ideal challenger. Tunney loved the science of boxing and studied films of Dempsey's fights, looking for a weakness. Outside the ring, the ex-marine quoted Shakespeare and was friends with Ernest Hemingway. The first Dempsey-Tunney fight, in 1926, drew more than 120,000 spectators, who saw Tunney skillfully outbox Dempsey and win a decision. When Dempsey's wife, actress Estelle Taylor, asked him why he lost, he replied, "Honey, I forgot to duck."

The rematch, on September 22, 1927, at Chicago's Soldier Field, made boxing history. Tunney controlled the opening rounds, but in the seventh, Dempsey suddenly knocked his foe to the canvas. Then, instead of obeying a then-local rule requiring that he go to a neutral corner, Dempsey loomed over Tunney, ready to resume the attack. The referee delayed starting his 10-count for a good five seconds while trying to steer Dempsey away. When his official count finally reached 9, which was arguably 14, Tunney got up. He survived the round, regained control of the fight, and eventually won on points. The "long count" debate—could Tunney have gotten up in 10?—would rage for years. But Dempsey, classy even in defeat, never questioned the result. "You were best," he told Tunney.

Gene Tunney (left) displays his championship form. Tunney retired the year after the "long count" fight with a 61-1-1 record.

As Tunney tries to recover, the referee directs Dempsey to a neutral corner. Dempsey gave up boxing a few months after the match.

Joe Louis, "the Brown Bomber," works out in 1937. Louis was heavyweight champion from 1937 to 1949, defending his title a record 25 times.

Louis-Schmeling: War in the Ring

On the eve of the 1938 rematch between American Joe Louis and German Max Schmeling, President Franklin D. Roosevelt told Louis, during a White House visit, "We need muscles like yours to beat Germany," showing that even as Nazi Germany moved toward war, a propaganda war was already raging in the boxing ring.

Louis, the first black heavyweight champion since Jack Johnson, seemed an unlikely hero for a frankly racist America. But unlike Johnson, he kept his feelings in check. Louis had started boxing as a teen, using money his mother gave him for violin lessons to pay for gym workouts. He moved up quickly, demolishing 27 consecutive opponents with a stinging left jab and powerful right.

Only Schmeling blocked Louis's path to a championship fight. Preparing for their 1936 encounter, Schmeling discovered that Louis would drop his guard after throwing a left jab and used the fault to beat him with a 12th-round KO. Nazi propaganda minister Joseph Goebbels invoked Hitler's name in a congratulatory telegram.

Louis was humiliated by the loss, his first as a pro. Even though he went on to knock out James Braddock in 1937 to become champion, Louis said, "I don't want nobody to call me champ until I beat Schmeling." The Louis-Schmeling rematch, on June 22, 1938, at Yankee Stadium, drew unprecedented attention. At the opening bell Louis attacked savagely, knocking out Schmeling just two minutes and four seconds into the fight. One blow broke two of Schmeling's vertebrae. When he cried out in pain, German technicians cut off radio transmission to the fatherland.

For Hitler the outcome was a bitter rebuff to his fantasies of racial supremacy. White America was content to see the matter as a triumph of American virtue over German evil. Louis and Schmeling eventually rose above the fray to develop a lifelong friendship.

Max Schmeling celebrates after knocking out Joe Louis in 1936. Schmeling became a Nazi propaganda tool—a symbol of alleged Aryan superiority—and was even invited to lunch with Hitler.

Louis pounds Schmeling during the rematch. Louis, a ferocious puncher, hit the German so hard he had to be hospitalized for 10 days before boarding his homebound ship carried on a stretcher.

Sugar Ray Robinson jabs at Jake LaMotta in the ninth round of their 1951 contest for the middle-weight title, the last fight of their epic rivalry.

Sugar Ray vs. the Bronx Bull

Sugar Ray Robinson and Jake LaMotta matched up six times during the 1940s and '50s, forming one of boxing's greatest rivalries. LaMotta once joked, "I fought Sugar Ray so often, I almost got diabetes."

Robinson was born Walker Smith Jr. He assumed his new name as a teenager in a Harlem gym when he used another fighter's boxing certificate. "Sugar" was added when a manager described his style as "sweet as sugar." Robinson won more than 80 fights as an amateur and began his welterweight pro career with 40 straight wins. He had lightning-fast hands and feet, a punishing left hook, and unparalleled defensive skills.

During his 25 years in the ring, Robinson weighed between 134 and 160 pounds and was commonly described as "pound-for-pound the best fighter ever." "He's the only one who was better than me," said heavyweight champ Muhammad Ali later. Outside the ring, Robinson lived high. He drove a pink Cadillac, owned a nightclub, and traveled with an entourage.

LaMotta grew up in the Bronx, a tough youngster whose father made him fight neighborhood kids to entertain other adults. After spending time in a reform school for petty crimes, LaMotta took up serious boxing. He was short for a middleweight—5 feet 8 inches—but his combative, brawling style quickly earned him victories and the nickname the Bronx Bull.

The Robinson-LaMotta rivalry began in 1942 when Robinson beat the heavier LaMotta on points. Four months later LaMotta handed Robinson his first defeat. But Robinson avenged the loss shortly afterward and then beat LaMotta twice more in the '40s. Robinson won the welterweight title in 1946; LaMotta took the middleweight crown in 1949. That set the stage for Robinson to move up a weight class and again challenge LaMotta. Nearly 15,000 spectators watched the fight live in Chicago Stadium on February 14, 1951. Across the nation, the new medium of television drew some 30 million fans to the flickering black-and-white spectacle. Robinson took control in the ninth. By the 13th, LaMotta was battered and bleeding, too weak to raise his hands. But he refused to go down, and the referee finally stopped the fight.

Over the next decade, Robinson lost and won back the middleweight title four times. Money problems forced him to fight into his mid-40s, but he later recouped some losses by acting in several movies. One of his final public appearances before he died in 1989 was as best man at LaMotta's wedding.

Rocky Marciano builds strong bones. The heavyweight champion, who finished with a record of 49 and 0, had a simple boxing style: "Just go in there and go crazy."

"The Rock" Rocks Jersey Joe

Long before "Got Milk?" was a popular advertising slogan, Rocky Marciano projected a wholesome image chugging a milk shake *(left)*. The 5-foot-10¼-inch 185-pounder was small for a heavyweight, but he made up for his size with relentless training and bullish determination. "He was the toughest, strongest, most dedicated fighter who ever wore gloves," wrote Red Smith. "Fear wasn't in his vocabulary and pain had no meaning."

Born Rocco Marchegiano, the son of Italian immigrants, he was a talented athlete who concentrated on boxing only after failing a minor-league baseball tryout. After turning pro at age 24, he trained by punching underwater to build strength and by throwing a football left-handed so his left would equal his mighty right, which he called Suzie Q. When he fought aging former champ Joe Louis in 1951, he knocked his boyhood idol out of the ring in the eighth round and wept.

A year later Marciano went up against world champion Jersey Joe Walcott in an epic battle at Philadelphia's Municipal Stadium. Though 38 years old, Walcott had just won the title he had pursued for years, and he was determined to keep it. He knocked Marciano down early and controlled the opening rounds. A bloody, exhausted Marciano knew his only chance was a knockout. Early in the 13th he unleashed one of the most devastating punches in boxing history—a short right to Walcott's chin. Walcott dropped to the canvas "like flour out a chute," as one writer put it.

Marciano successfully defended his title six times, including a 1955 fight with Archie Moore in which Moore said he felt like "someone had been . . . hitting you with rocks." At his mother's urging Marciano retired, the only undefeated heavyweight champion in history. Revered for clean living as a fighter, he wasn't so pious in retirement. He partied with alleged Mafia figures and died in a 1969 small-plane crash with a reputed mobster's nephew.

Rocky Marciano tangles with Jersey Joe Walcott on September 23, 1952. He lands a savage right (middle) in the 13th round, sending Walcott down for the count. Despite the challenger's unbeaten streak, champion Walcott had been disdainful before the fight: "If I lose," he said, "take my name out of the record books."

Ali "Rumbles" With Foreman

Muhammad Ali mastered the art of self-promotion like no other athlete. As a 12-year-old he knocked on neighborhood doors to announce his upcoming fights. By the time he fought George Foreman two decades later, in 1974's "Rumble in the Jungle," he was one of the world's best-known figures.

Born Cassius Marcellus Clay Jr., he began boxing at a policeman's suggestion. In 1960, at age 18, he won Olympic gold. He was amazingly quick with his hands, feet—and mouth. He talked in rhymes ("Float like a butterfly, sting like a bee / You can't hit what you can't see"). He also managed to back up an outrageous claim—"I am The Greatest"—by beating Sonny Liston in 1964 for the heavyweight crown.

Immediately after the fight Clay announced that he had joined the Nation of Islam—the Black Muslims—and changed his name. He subsequently refused induction into the army on religious grounds. He was stripped of his title and didn't fight again for nearly four years. Vindicated by the Supreme Court, he resumed fighting but lost a decision to Joe Frazier in a classic 1971 championship brawl.

Three years later the title was held by undefeated George Foreman, and promoter Don King set up a fight between him and Ali in Zaire. Ali pumped up the prefight hype, befriending local children, mugging for the cameras, and taunting Foreman. The bout began at 4 a.m. for a U.S. prime-time TV audience. A crowd of nearly 60,000 Zairians, mostly Ali partisans, chanted, "*A-li, booma-ya*! (Ali, kill him!)"

But Ali surprised everyone. Simply leaning against the ropes *(left)*, he blocked or ducked Foreman's blows, a strategy he later dubbed "rope-a-dope." By the fourth round, Foreman was tiring. "Is that the best you can do?" Ali jibed. In the fifth Ali declared, "Now it's my turn" and began hammering away. In the eighth he knocked Foreman to the canvas with a quick left-right combination and reclaimed the heavyweight title.

After letting George Foreman punch himself arm-weary in their October 30, 1974, fight, Muhammad Ali levels his opponent (above).

A spent Foreman is counted out. Ali had boasted, "When I hit that Foreman, it's going to be the launching of the first colored satellite."

Ali vs. Frazier: "The Thrilla in Manila"

Muhammad Ali and Joe Frazier fought three times during the 1970s—not counting an impromptu brawl in a television studio triggered by Ali's insult, "You're ignorant, Joe." Their enmity was so bitter that even two decades later Frazier would say, "I still want to take him apart piece by piece and send him back to Jesus."

The feud had started in 1971 with a match in Madison Square Garden. Both men were undefeated. Ali's nearly four-year exile during the Vietnam War had slowed him, but he still mixed fancy footwork with a powerful punch. Frazier, who had become champion in Ali's absence, was a relentless brawler. Ali tried to slug it out with Frazier, and in the 15th Frazier dropped him with a left hook to the jaw. Ali struggled to his feet and finished the match but lost the decision.

Their 1974 rematch was anticlimactic, for by this time Frazier had lost the title to George Foreman. Ali won a decision while taunting Frazier with "You're soooo ugly," thereby setting the tone for their rubber match a year later—after Ali had beaten Foreman to regain the title (page 93).

Ali was riding high in 1975 when he met Frazier in Manila, Philippines. He called Frazier "the Gorilla," punched a little toy gorilla he kept in his pocket, and chanted, "It'll be a thrilla, a killa, a chilla when I get the Gorilla in Manila." Frazier responded, "I want to take his heart out." Around the world, some 700 million TV viewers tuned in.

Ali controlled the early rounds, battering his opponent. Frazier took over the middle rounds, attacking Ali's body with both hands. By the 10th round, Ali's corner man begged him to "go down to the well once more!" Ali responded with savage right-hand blows. In the 13th, he sent Frazier's bloody mouthpiece flying into the crowd. After the 14th, Frazier was barely able to see through swollen eyes, and his trainer threw in the towel.

The boxers grudgingly offered each other respect, though no warmth. "It was like death," said Ali. "Closest thing to dyin' that I know of." Said Frazier: "Lawdy, Lawdy, he's a great champion. I hit him with punches that would bring down the walls of a city."

Muhammad Ali connects with a right against "Smokin' Joe" Frazier on October 13, 1975, in the Philippines. Ali retained his title in the brutal match.

Ali, postfight: "You get so tired. It makes you go a little insane. It's so painful."

"It was like death."

Muhammad Ali, after "The Thrilla in Manila"

Frazier's battered face. "No one will ever forget what you did here," his trainer said.

Leonard vs. Duran: "No Mas! No Mas!"

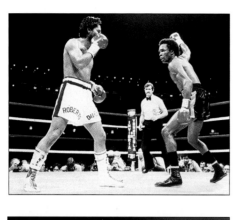

Sugar Ray Leonard winds up his right, faking a bolo punch against Roberto Duran (top), taunts Duran (above), and connects (below). Leonard regained his welterweight championship in the November 25, 1980, fight when Duran just sat down.

He was born Ray Charles Leonard, named for the great rhythm-and-blues singer, but after he started boxing at 13, people dubbed him Sugar Ray because his flashy style reminded them of another superstar, Sugar Ray Robinson *(pages 88-89)*. In 1976 Leonard won an Olympic gold medal and shortly afterward went pro, defeating Wilfred Benitez in 1979 to become welterweight champion.

He then signed to defend his title against the fearsome Roberto Duran in June 1980 in Montreal. Duran, a Panamanian national hero known for his *manos de piedra* (hands of stone), snarled insults at Leonard during the fight, worked inside to counter Leonard's speed, and won a close match, continuing to sneer at his opponent even after the decision was announced.

The rematch, just five months later in New Orleans, was another story. The differences from the first fight began early when, instead of some local singer droning the national anthem, the audience heard Ray Charles's stirring rendition of "America the Beautiful." Leonard then put on his own performance, dancing circles around Duran, neutralizing his brawling attacks, and hitting him with vicious jabs. Remembering Montreal, Leonard missed no chance to taunt and humiliate Duran. Then, in the eighth round, the audience and the boxing world were stunned when a dispirited Duran suddenly turned his back on Leonard and said to the referee, "*No mas! No mas!* (No more! No more!)" Duran complained of stomach cramps, but nobody was buying. "I made him quit," said Leonard. "I outclassed him and frustrated him. I made him look like a fool."

Leonard suffered an eye injury in 1982 and began a cycle of retirements and comebacks, including a brilliant performance against Marvin Hagler in 1987 to win the middleweight title. He built a fortune from his ring earnings and savvy investments, but his ego drove him to keep boxing, until his career finally ended at age 40 with a humiliating loss to Hector Camacho.

Claiming stomach cramps, Duran has ice applied to his belly. After the fight, irate Panamanian fans threw rocks at his home.

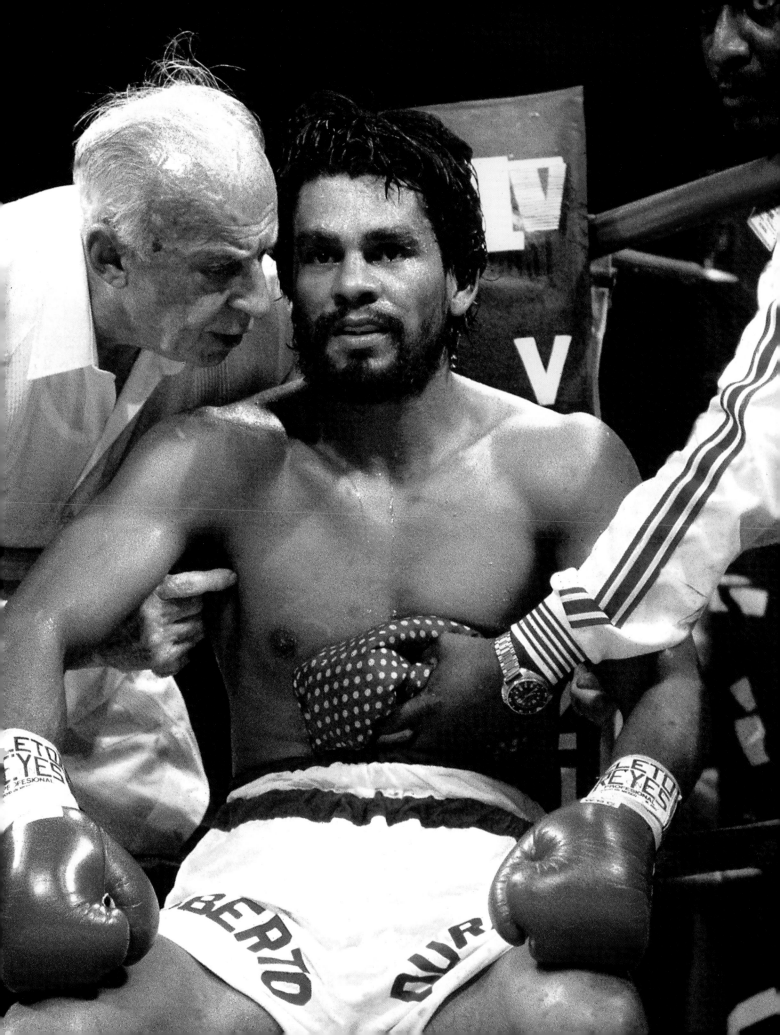

The "Bite of the Century"

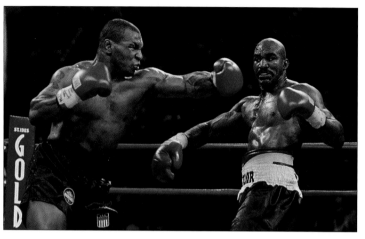

"Iron Mike" Tyson swings futilely at Evander Holyfield in their June 28, 1997, fight. A frustrated Tyson erupted in rage and bit both of Holyfield's ears. He was disqualified, pandemonium ensued, and 40 spectators were injured.

"Madman! A crazed Mike Tyson disgraces himself and his sport."

Cover of *Sports Illustrated*

When 17-year-old Mike Tyson failed to make the 1984 U.S. Olympic team, he left the arena and used a nearby tree as a punching bag. It was a sign of things to come. Tyson grew up in Brooklyn, New York, with "an alcoholic and a pimp for parents," as he would later say. By age 12, he had been arrested 30 times for crimes as serious as armed robbery. He was sent to a reform school in upstate New York, where the boxing coach took one look at him and got in touch with Cus D'Amato, who had trained former heavyweight champion Floyd Patterson and ran a nearby gym. When D'Amato first saw young Tyson in the ring, he predicted, "That's the heavyweight champion of the world." Under D'Amato's tutelage, Tyson developed explosive power to go with an inborn savagery.

Though only 18 when he turned pro, Tyson was intimidating. He had a size 19 neck and packed 225 pounds of sculpted muscle on a hulking 5-foot-11-inch frame. He destroyed his first 27 opponents, 25 by knockout. When he met then-champ Trevor Berbick in late 1986, it was more of the same. "I saw the fear in his eyes," said Tyson after knocking out Berbick in round 2. At 20, Tyson was the youngest heavyweight titleholder ever.

But his private life was a mess. His brief marriage to actress Robin Givens ended under a cloud of domestic-abuse allegations. He crashed a car into a tree and had minor run-ins with the law. Then, shortly after an unknown named James "Buster" Douglas dethroned him with a KO in 1990, Tyson was convicted of raping an 18-year-old beauty pageant contestant and spent nearly four years in prison. He resumed fighting after being paroled but was beaten by Evander Holyfield in a 1996 title fight.

Their 1997 rematch was a spectacle. Celebrities paid thousands of dollars for ringside seats at the sold-out MGM Grand in Las Vegas. Early in the fight, Tyson complained that a Holyfield head butt had opened a gash above his eye. In the third round, he boiled over. Spitting out his mouthpiece, he bit off a piece of Holyfield's right ear. As Holyfield recoiled, the referee, incredibly, stopped the fight for only a moment to warn Tyson, and then let the boxers resume. Within seconds Tyson bit off the tip of Holyfield's other ear. This time he was disqualified and his boxing license suspended.

At first Tyson apologized, but in 1998 he punched and kicked two motorists after a minor traffic accident and spent three months in jail. Nonetheless, his boxing license was reinstated. About biting Holyfield his words were defiant: "I would do it again," he said, "if a referee failed to protect me."

Evander Holyfield winces in pain after being bitten by Mike Tyson. "I have to retaliate," said Tyson, by way of explaining himself.

A Game for a Fast-Moving Age

★

100 YEARS OF BASKETBALL

I n late 1891 Dr. James Naismith *(inset),* a physical education instructor in Springfield, Massachusetts, pondered how he might keep his YMCA class active during the cold winter ahead. After some thought, on December 21 he posted 13 rules for a new game. He then sent a janitor in search of two square boxes.

The man came back with round peach baskets instead. After he nailed them to the lower rail of the gymnasium balcony, which happened to be exactly 10 feet high, Naismith divided his class of 18 into two teams and handed the players a soccer ball. Basketball was born.

There have been a few changes since. Most basically, the value of a field goal has increased from one to two points, the number of players per side has been cut to five, and dribbling, initially forbidden, is now permitted. But the game still retains the inherent simplicity of Naismith's vision. And because of that, for over a century it has served as a showcase for everything good and everything contradictory about sports—teamwork and individual accomplishment, careful planning and instant reflex, dynasties and dramatic upsets, power and finesse—qualities personified by such modern stars of the games as Larry Bird and Magic Johnson *(right).*

If basketball were music, wrote Michael Novak in 1988, it would be jazz: "improvisatory,

Nearly a century after James Naismith dreamed up basketball, two of its greatest stars—Earvin "Magic" Johnson of the Los Angeles Lakers and Larry Bird of the Boston Celtics—battle for a rebound.

The NBA's first marquee star, bespectacled George Mikan of Minneapolis, goes strong to the hoop. The center was so well known that before a 1948 game in New York the sign outside Madison Square Garden read "George Mikan vs. Knicks."

Harlem Globetrotter Reece "Goose" Tatum hilariously distracts a gullible opponent while "hiding" the ball. The gangly Tatum, who had an 84-inch wingspan, was the linchpin of the Trotters' zany routines from 1942 to 1955.

free, individualistic, corporate, sweaty, fast, exulting, screeching, torrid, explosive." The greatest hits of its best performers are included in the following pages.

The First Standouts. College basketball was the dominant form of the sport during the first half-century, so it's not surprising that one of the earliest stars was not a pro. He was Hank Luisetti, who played for Stanford University in the 1930s. Able to pass behind his back, fake while in midair, and shoot on the run with one hand instead of using the then-universal two-hand set shot, Luisetti was a true revolutionary, the first modern player.

The early game had some professional teams, but few managed to survive the Depression. The best were the Sphas (short for the South Philadelphia Hebrew Association), who won seven American Basketball League titles in 13 years, and the all-black New York Rens, who took their name from the Renaissance Casino in Harlem. By far the most popular team, however, was the Harlem Globetrotters. Founded in 1926 by Abe Saperstein, an immigrant from England with keen business sense, the Globetrotters were more than a match for any other pro team. Their stars —Nat "Sweetwater" Clifton, Marques Haynes, Reece "Goose" Tatum *(inset)*, Meadowlark Lemon, and Curly Neal—became household names.

They also delivered an important message to white America: "Blacks are playing basketball," as Saperstein put it in 1948. "You are going to see this game black." And sure enough, two years later Earl Lloyd of West Virginia State College became the first African American to play in a National Basketball Association (NBA) game.

The league was only four years old, and 6-foot-10 George Mikan *(left, top)* was its superstar, the first of a new breed of agile, athletic big men. Mikan led the Minneapolis Lakers to championships in six of their first seven seasons, becoming the NBA's first scoring champion and truly dominant player. "He could raise that left elbow and move to the basket, and the bodies would just start to fly," said Swede Carlson, a teammate. Mikan was so hard to defend, in fact, that the league doubled the width of the foul lane in 1951. Another tactic—stalling to keep the ball out of his hands —made the game so boring that in 1954 the league instituted a 24-second clock to speed up the action and hype scoring. In the end, though, it wasn't rule changes but the constant physical

Laker great Elgin Baylor, owner of the NBA's third highest all-time scoring average, drives to the basket. Defending against him, said an opponent, was "like guarding a flood."

Bob Cousy keys a Celtic fast break with a long pass. Once benched in college for "flashy" play, Cousy led the NBA in assists eight times.

Boston coach Red Auerbach lights up a trademark victory cigar. The stogy, said Bill Russell, "was part of what made the Celtics who we were."

punishment, including two broken legs, three broken fingers, a broken wrist, a broken nose, and dozens of stitches, that forced Mikan's retirement in 1954.

The void Mikan left was considerable, but it was eventually filled by a 6-foot-5-inch forward named Elgin Baylor *(page 103),* one of the first players to use basketball as a stage for athletic artistry. He began playing for Minneapolis in 1958. "Watching Elgin Baylor on a basketball court was like watching Gene Kelly in the rain," wrote columnist Jim Murray. In 1960 the Lakers moved to Los Angeles, and Baylor scored 71 points in a game. During a 14-year career, when he teamed with Jerry West to form one of basketball's greatest one-two punches, he averaged 27.4 points and 13.5 rebounds a contest. Yet he never won an NBA title—losing seven times to the most successful team in NBA history, the Boston Celtics.

The Shamrock Dynasty. Teamwork was the Celtics' hallmark. Boston coach Red Auerbach *(left, bottom)* believed in it so fervently he once berated a player for not sharing a pregame candy bar. And it led to the Celtics' winning 11 championships in 13 years during the 1950s and '60s, including eight in a row.

The dynasty began in 1956 when Bill Russell joined Bob Cousy on the squad. Cousy *(left, top),* a physically unprepossessing 6-foot-1 guard, was an offensive magician who dazzled with behind-the-back passes and an uncanny ability to find the open man. Russell *(number 6, right),* a 6-foot-9 center, changed the game with his defense. He rebounded, triggered the fast break, and made shot blocking an art form long before it became an official statistic. Just the "sound of his footsteps," said Auerbach, intimidated opposing players.

Russell, Cousy, Sam Jones, K. C. Jones, Bill Sharman, Tommy Heinsohn —they never tired of winning. "We'd come back for training camp every year with saliva dripping off our lips, saying, 'Kill, kill, kill, I want another title,' " recalled Cousy. The beat went on even after Cousy retired in 1963. John Havlicek *(number 17, right)* stepped in, first gaining fame by coming off the bench as the best sixth man in league history. Havlicek's most memorable play came in game 7 of the 1965 Eastern Division Finals against Philadelphia. He intercepted an inbounds pass to seal the win as Celtics radio announcer Johnny Most, spent by the nonstop action, croaked, "Havlicek stole the ball! It's all over! Johnny Havlicek stole the ball!"

Russell, though, was the mainstay during the Celtic glory years. He used

Bill Russell (6) and John Havlicek (17) leap for a rebound in front of Warriors superstar Wilt Chamberlain. The rivalry between Russell and Chamberlain was so intense they didn't become friends until long after their playing days were over.

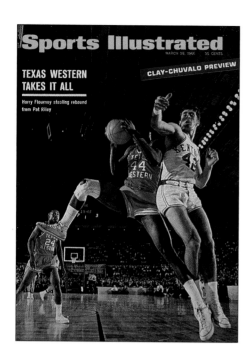

Harry Flourney, one of Texas Western's all-black starting five, steals a rebound from Kentucky's Pat Riley—a future NBA Coach of the Year—in the 1966 NCAA title game.

Houston's Elvin Hayes shoots over UCLA's Lew Alcindor during their 1968 classic in the Astrodome. Hayes swished two free throws with 28 seconds remaining to snap UCLA's 47-game winning streak.

selfless play to become the NBA's Most Valuable Player five times, and his match-ups against Wilt Chamberlain *(number 13, page 105)* stand among the greatest the game has ever seen. The two met for the first time during Chamberlain's rookie season in 1959. Chamberlain scored 30 points. Russell had 35 rebounds. Boston won. It was the start of a fierce rivalry—and a pattern.

Chamberlain was huge, at 7 feet 1 inch and 275 pounds, and astoundingly agile. Able to score with fadeaway jump shots as well as thunderous dunks, he *averaged* 50.4 points a game in 1962, hitting a record 100 against the New York Knicks on March 2. A four-time MVP, he was also the league's perennial rebounding leader—and once even led in assists.

"He was the best player of all time because he dominated both ends of the floor like nobody else ever could," Russell said. But Chamberlain was fated to play bridesmaid to the Celtic great. Russell's team went 86-57 in their meetings and won seven titles—compared with none for Chamberlain's teams—during the players' rivalry. Russell capped his career by succeeding the retiring Auerbach in 1966 to become the first African American coach in NBA history.

The College Game's Fall and Rebirth. In
the early 1950s college basketball was still flying high, with great players and memorable teams. Then, suddenly, it all came crashing down. Thirty-two players from seven schools, including stars from the nation's best teams, admitted to aiding gamblers by shaving points in certain games. One of the fixers, All-American Gene Melchiorre of Bradley, offered a simple explanation: "None of us had any money." In the scandal's wake some schools withdrew from big-time basketball. The college game was a long time recovering.

Instrumental in that recovery was coach John Wooden and his UCLA Bruins of the 1960s and early '70s. Wooden, a former All-American at Purdue, endlessly preached his "Pyramid of Success" building blocks, including cooperation and self-control. In 1964, without a starter taller than 6 feet 5, the Bruins went 30-0 and won their first NCAA title. During the next 11 seasons, UCLA would win nine more championships.

One year the Bruins didn't prevail was 1966, when Texas Western (now the University of Texas at El Paso) became the first NCAA champion to start five African Americans *(left, top)*. After the Miners upset an all-white

Kentucky team coached by Adolph Rupp in the finals, Texas Western coach Don Haskins received 40,000 pieces of hate mail, but his team had earned a place in history. "You guys got a lot of black kids scholarships around this country," he told his players. "You helped change the world a little bit."

The next year, 7-foot-2-inch center Lew Alcindor—who later became Kareem Abdul-Jabbar—scored 56 points in his first game for UCLA. The Bruins went on a remarkable streak, winning seven straight NCAA titles. One of their few setbacks came during the 1968-69 season. A huge television audience and 52,693 spectators at the Astrodome watched Elvin Hayes score 39 points for the University of Houston (opposite, bottom) and end UCLA's 47-game winning streak. UCLA got revenge two months later in the NCAA tourney, stifling Hayes and taking another title.

After Alcindor went on to the NBA, Bill Walton led UCLA to more titles in the early 1970s. In the 1973 championship game, the first to be televised in prime time, Walton made 21 of 22 attempts and scored 44 points. Two years later Wooden won his last championship (inset, opposite) and retired with an incredible .804 winning percentage.

The 1980s and 1990s were marked by dominant programs at Duke, North Carolina, and Kentucky and an influx of cash from TV. The NCAA tournament was dubbed March Madness, and Final Four tickets became precious, no doubt helped by the kind of drama that unfolded when unheralded North Carolina State met top-ranked Houston's racehorse team—nicknamed Phi Slamma Jamma—in the 1983 title game (right, top). The Cougars' Hakeem Olajuwon and Clyde Drexler, future NBA superstars, could only look on as the Wolfpack won when a 35-foot prayer was grabbed and slammed home at the buzzer. Mop-haired coach Jim Valvano, who a decade later would die of cancer at the age of 47, left an indelible image as he raced onto the court looking for someone—anyone—to hug.

Women, like men, had played college basketball practically since the game's beginnings, but under such stultifying rules that even the number of

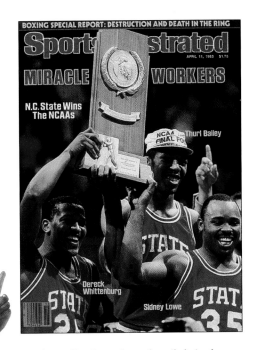

North Carolina State players happily hoist the NCAA trophy after beating the high-flying Houston Cougars 54-52 for the 1983 championship. The last-second upset helped make the Final Four as popular as the World Series and the Super Bowl.

"Had the league been around 10 years ago, Cheryl would have been Michael, Magic, and Larry all wrapped into one."

NBA star Reggie Miller, on his sister

Freshman Cheryl Miller raises her arms in triumph after leading USC to the 1983 NCAA title. A year later, Miller paced the United States to an Olympic gold medal.

Jerry West of the Los Angeles Lakers drives to the hoop with a move that became the model for the NBA logo. When his playing days ended, he proved an all-star executive for the Lakers.

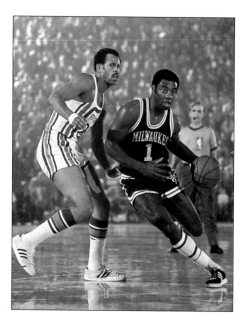

Oscar Robertson flashes past a defender en route to the 1971 NBA title. A big man with a dead shot and incredibly nimble moves, he became the prototype of large NBA guards to come.

their dribbles was limited until 1966. Only after Title IX was passed in 1972 did women play for a national collegiate championship. Then sports fans came to know such stars as Ann Meyers, a brilliant passer and shooter from UCLA who earned an NBA tryout; Nancy Lieberman, who went on to play for a minor-league men's team; Lynette Woodard, the first black women's star and a future Globetrotter; and Cheryl Miller *(inset, page 107)*, still considered the best women's player of all time.

Miller led USC to two national titles in the early 1980s and was three-time college Player of the Year. Upon graduation she seemed a sure bet for pro superstardom. "No woman would have been able to stop her," said her brother Reggie, an NBA All-Star. Unfortunately, there was no serious women's pro league for her to step into. By the time the WNBA started in 1997, Miller was in her 30s, her knees were sore, and she had to be content with coaching.

Mr. Clutch, the Big O, and Dr. J. Wilt Chamberlain wasn't the only NBA star overshadowed by the dominant Celtics of the 1960s. Jerry West *(left, top)* and Oscar Robertson *(left, bottom),* two of the game's greatest players, had to wait until the early 1970s, near the end of their careers, to win titles.

As a boy, West shot baskets on a dirt court outside his West Virginia home until his fingers cracked and bled. In the NBA the agile 6-foot-3-inch forward-guard became known as Mr. Clutch for his ability to make shots when the pressure was on—like the 60-foot buzzer-beater he sank against the New York Knicks in 1970. But his Lakers lost eight of the nine times they played in the NBA Finals during his 14-year career, and six of the defeats were at the hands of the Celtics. West's lone championship came in 1972, when he teamed with Wilt Chamberlain to sweep the Knicks. The title capped a dream season in which West was named MVP and the Lakers won a record 33 straight games. Their 69-13 season mark set a record that stood for over 20 years—until the 1995-96 Chicago Bulls *(page 120)* went 72-10.

Oscar Robertson, West's teammate on the 1960 U.S. Olympic team, was the game's first big guard at 6 feet 5 inches and 215 pounds. He was so far ahead of his time as an all-around player that basketball lacked phrases to describe his feats. In 1961, for example, before anyone knew what to call a "triple-double" (reaching double digits in scoring, rebounding, and assists in a single game), Robertson *averaged* a triple double—30.8 points, 12.5

rebounds, and 11.4 assists—for an entire season. No one has come close since. "He is so great, he scares me," Red Auerbach once said of the Big O. In 1971, after being traded from the Cincinnati Royals to the Milwaukee Bucks, Robertson teamed up with young pro Lew Alcindor and swept to the NBA crown. Said Robertson of the locker-room championship celebration, "This is the first champagne I've ever had, and it tastes mighty sweet."

The New York Knicks, winners of NBA championships in 1970 and 1973 *(right)*, gave new meaning to the term "smart basketball." Forward Bill Bradley was a Princeton grad and Rhodes scholar. Forward Jerry Lucas had astounding recall, once even memorizing the Manhattan phone book. Reserve Phil Jackson was a student of Eastern mysticism. With quick-witted playmaking guard Walt Frazier, rock-solid center Willis Reed, defensive whiz Dave DeBusschere, and shot-making genius Earl "the Pearl" Monroe—on board for the '73 title—they formed "the ultimate team," Lucas said.

Watching the NBA's success, some would-be sports moguls decided to try for a piece of the action. In 1967 they hired George Mikan, a smart basketball man in his own right, to become the first commissioner of a new league, the American Basketball Association (ABA). Hoping to win a network TV contract, Mikan dreamed up the idea of using a red, white, and blue ball, which became the ABA's signature. Though one coach said that the ball looked as if it "belongs on the nose of a seal," the new league had a lot of appeal. It featured a loose, fast, playgroundlike game with crowd-pleasing slam dunks, a three-point shot (an ABA invention), and plenty of scoring. Stars such as Rick Barry *(left, in an NBA uniform)*, Moses Malone, and George Gervin went up against the revolutionary, game-transforming acrobatics of Julius "Dr. J" Erving, the ABA's marquee player *(right)*. Even so, the league never got its network deal and folded in 1976, the NBA taking in its four strongest franchises.

Some of the pillars of the New York Knicks— from left, Jerry Lucas, Walt Frazier, Willis Reed, Phil Jackson, and Bill Bradley—celebrate after winning their second title in 1973.

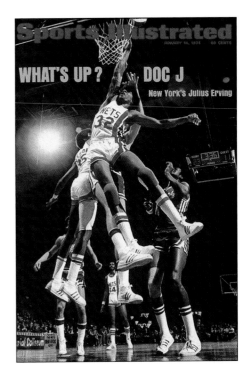

Julius "Dr. J" Erving operates for the New York Nets in 1974. The ABA sank in 1976, but Erving soared in the NBA for another 11 years.

Rick Barry shoots an underhanded free throw in 1972. Despite his outdated style, he was among the all-time best free-throw shooters.

That NBA Magic. The 1979 NCAA title game was one of those rare sports events anticipated by the entire nation, and for one reason—the match-up between two of the greatest players in the history of college hoops. Magic Johnson of Michigan State faced Larry Bird of Indiana State in a game that garnered the highest TV ratings in the tournament's history. When the pair brought their game to the NBA the following year, they kicked off a fabulous new era in pro basketball. Their huge talent, unselfish play, brilliant court sense, and fierce showdowns helped to almost double NBA attendance during their careers—and inspired other players to raise the level of their game. Said Chris Mullin, who played both against and with Bird and Johnson: "They set a precedent . . . play every game hard."

Bird, a shy, self-described "hick from French Lick [Indiana]," personified the scrappy play of the Boston Celtics. The 6-foot-9 forward dove for loose balls, sank three-pointers, and made no-look passes to such teammates as Kevin McHale and Robert Parish. He averaged 24.3 points a game during his career, was league MVP three straight times (1984-86), and led the Celtics to three titles. During the 1985-86 season Bird's team was nearly unbeatable on Boston Garden's famous parquet floor, going an NBA record 40-1 at home. The Celtics' one loss, of course, was to Johnson's Los Angeles Lakers.

Magic's flashy ball handling and Hollywood smile embodied the "Showtime" Lakers *(page 113)*. At 6 feet 9 inches he was the tallest point guard in NBA history. Johnson spearheaded the electric L.A. fast break —"I can still see him in my head coming up court," said Bird later, "and it still pisses me off." He was league MVP three times and paced the Lakers to five titles during the 1980s. But his legendary duels against Bird—they met on the court 37 times as pros—defined his career. Said Johnson, "People who saw our games against each other saw some of the best basketball ever played."

The same could be said for anyone fortunate enough to watch Michael Jordan of the Chicago Bulls. A star at the University of North Carolina whose jump shot beat Georgetown for the 1982 NCAA championship and a leader of the U.S. Olympic team that won gold in 1984, the lithe 6-foot-6-inch Jordan was named NBA Rookie of the Year in 1985 and quickly emerged as the league's most dangerous player and one of the world's most popular personalities. In 1991 he led the Bulls to the first of what would ultimately be six NBA championships in the decade *(pages 120-123)*.

NBA players were allowed to compete in the Olympics for the first

---

Manute Bol (7 feet 7) and Tyrone "Muggsy" Bogues (5 feet 3) were the tallest and shortest players in NBA history—and teammates for Washington in the late 1980s.

time the following year. The United States, whose only Olympic losses had come in a controversial 1972 decision *(page 174)* and a frustrating 1988 effort, assembled a "Dream Team" consisting of Jordan, one college star, and 10 more of the best players in NBA history, including Johnson, Bird, Karl Malone of the Utah Jazz, Patrick Ewing of the New York Knicks, David Robinson of the San Antonio Spurs, and Jordan's teammate Scottie Pippen *(right)*. In Barcelona, where they were mobbed by worshipful fans whenever they appeared in public, they overwhelmed their Olympic foes, winning their eight games by an average margin of 44 points as a television audience of some three billion people in 180 countries eagerly tuned in. The gold medal ceremony brought a surge of patriotic spirit. "It was the most awesome feeling I've ever had," said Johnson. "Goose bumps just came all over my body."

The men's team overshadowed the American women, who came home disappointed with a bronze medal after winning gold in 1984 and 1988. But led by college stars Lisa Leslie, Teresa Edwards, and Rebecca Lobo, the United States bounced back in 1996. Playing in front of huge crowds in the Georgia Dome in Atlanta, they swept to the gold in Dream Team-like fashion, attracting multitudes of new fans to the women's game and serving as a catalyst for the creation of a new women's professional league, the WNBA.

Cynthia Cooper *(right, bottom)* wasn't expected to star when she joined the Houston Comets for the league's debut season the following year. She had been a role player for the Cheryl Miller-led USC champions of the early 1980s and had then spent 11 years playing in Europe. But using a three-point shot and a jump hook she had refined overseas, the 5-foot-10-inch guard quickly proved herself to be the WNBA's Michael Jordan, leading the league in scoring and pacing the Comets to the title three years in a row. Along with fellow stars Leslie, Lobo, Edwards, and Sheryl Swoopes, she helped the WNBA attract an average of more than 10,000 fans per game—double what league officials had originally projected.

As the final buzzer sounded on the 20th century, the WNBA expanded to 16 teams. The men's league, with its 29 teams, attracted more than 20 million spectators. Dr. Naismith's invention during the infancy of the telephone was more popular than ever in an Internet world, as a quarter-billion people around the globe practiced this American-born sport. Featured on the following pages are epic teams and immortal players who took the modern game to unimaginable heights with dazzling displays of individual skill, teamwork, and competitive fire.

The 1992 Olympic "Dream Team": left to right, front row, Scottie Pippen, John Stockton, and Clyde Drexler; center row, Larry Bird, Michael Jordan, coach Chuck Daly, Charles Barkley, and Chris Mullin; back row, Patrick Ewing, college star Christian Laettner, Magic Johnson, David Robinson, and Karl Malone.

Cynthia Cooper, the WNBA's first superstar, goes to the hoop in 1997. Other women's pro leagues had fizzled; the WNBA sizzled.

The Lakers' Kareem Abdul-Jabbar prepares to stuff the ball home in a 1989 game against Phoenix as Showtime costars (left to right) James Worthy, Byron Scott, and Magic Johnson look on.

Showtime at the Fabulous Forum

Scantily clad Laker Girl cheerleaders pranced on the sidelines. Showbiz personalities like Jack Nicholson and Johnny Carson yelled their approval. Coach Pat Riley (page 106) slicked back his hair. And Magic Johnson (inset) led a dazzling fast break. During the 1980s this was the scene at the Los Angeles Forum. This was the brand of basketball called Showtime.

Showtime opened its decade-long run during the 1979-80 season when Johnson—fresh from leading Michigan State to the NCAA title (page 110)—and Kareem Abdul-Jabbar sparked the Lakers to their first NBA championship of the 1980s. The towering Abdul-Jabbar wielded his unique "sky hook," which Riley called, somewhat extravagantly, "the most awesome weapon in the history of any sport." Johnson was an ebullient guard whose smile lit up the Forum. His passion for the game dated to his childhood. "I dribbled to the store with my right hand and back with my left hand," Johnson recalled. "Then I slept with my basketball." So versatile was he that in the decisive game of the 1980 Finals, he stepped in at center for an injured Abdul-Jabbar and scored 42 points.

The Lakers were fun to watch. After getting an outlet pass from Abdul-Jabbar, Johnson would race up the court with his head up and eyes scanning the floor. Then he would either find high-flying James Worthy slashing to the basket or toss a pass to Byron Scott spotting up for an outside shot or drive to the hoop himself. "We couldn't stop the avalanche," said Boston Celtic Danny Ainge after one bitter loss to Los Angeles. The Showtime Lakers won five NBA titles, including two over the Larry Bird-led Celtics.

Abdul-Jabbar hung up his shoes in 1989, at the age of 42, after winning six MVP awards and scoring an NBA-record 38,387 points, an average of 24.6 points per game. Johnson, a three-time MVP, announced he was HIV positive in 1991 and also retired. He returned briefly five years later, but it wasn't the same. The celebrities still came and the Laker Girls still danced, but Showtime was over.

Julius Erving takes flight. Dr. J's artistic, rousing dunks, delivered during 16 seasons in the ABA and NBA, changed the way the game was played.

High-Flying Masters of Slam

Derisively referred to as a "duffer shot" during the 1940s, frowned upon in the '50s, and actually banned outright in college ball for eight seasons between 1967 and 1976, the dunk required a little getting used to on the part of basketball fans. But then a young jam artist by the name of Julius Erving *(left)* took the world by storm.

In 1976, at the first-ever All-Star Game Slam Dunk Contest (another ABA innovation), Dr. J threw down the most memorable dunk in history. After dribbling the length of the court, he went airborne at the foul line and soared toward the hoop, holding the ball in one hand. That image of the Doctor—his Afro bobbing and red-and-white Converse sneakers flashing as he took the game far above the rim—inspired a generation of players. The slam has since become an integral part of basketball, a punctuation mark to fast breaks, alley-oop passes, and slick one-on-one moves. Like jazz, wrote *Sports Illustrated*, it has become an American art form.

Philadelphia 76er Darryl Dawkins shattered backboards with slam dunks twice in a 22-day span in 1979. He christened his first dunk, which rained glass bits down on Bill Robinzine of the Kansas City Kings, the Chocolate-Thunder-Flying, Robinzine-Crying, Teeth-Shaking, Glass-Breaking, Rump-Roasting, Bun-Toasting, Wham-Bam, Glass-Breaker-I-Am Jam. The NBA answered with collapsible, snap-back rims.

In the 1986 NBA All-Star Game Slam Dunk Contest, Spud Webb proved that dunking isn't just for big guys. Webb, only 5 feet 7, used his remarkable 42-inch vertical leap and imaginative moves to win the event.

Michael Jordan *(right)*, generally acknowledged as basketball's greatest player, may also have been its finest dunker. In a memorable contest with Dominique Wilkins *(right, top)*, the 6-foot-6 guard showed that he had the moves of Erving, the power of Dawkins, and the leaping ability of Webb. Jordan's flights—his tongue hanging out, ball in one hand, arms and legs spread wide—were so transcendent that the image became the logo for his line of Nike sneakers. Like any artist, however, Jordan couldn't explain all of his work. "I don't plan all that stuff," he said. "It just somehow happens naturally."

Air Jordan slams with authority. Jordan's dunks mesmerized even teammates. Said one: "I found myself just wanting to stop and watch him—and I was playing."

Atlanta's Dominique Wilkins soars like a Hawk. The eight-time All-Star forward was nicknamed the Human Highlight Film for his flashy play and became one of the NBA's all-time top scorers.

All-Powerful Rulers of the Paint

The Minneapolis Lakers in 1949 had too much of a good thing. They had 6-foot-7-inch, 230-pound Vern Mikkelsen, a former collegiate All-American, and 6-foot-10-inch George Mikan, the game's dominant player. But they didn't need two centers. So coach John Kundla turned Mikkelsen toward the basket, making him the first power forward. In doing so, he changed the game forever.

Ever since, basketball—or at least the bump-and-grind part of the game played in the brightly painted free-throw lane—has been ruled by forwards and centers noted more for girth than for grace. Wes Unseld was one. Barely 6 feet 7 but a solid 245 pounds, he was a relentless rebounder who set bone-jarring picks and held his own against taller centers, earning league MVP honors in 1969 and leading the Washington Bullets to an NBA title in 1978.

Moses Malone and Charles Barkley also fit the mold. Malone, a three-time MVP, led the league in rebounding six times during one seven-year span and played an NBA record 1,207 straight games without fouling out. Barkley, the "Round Mound of Rebound" in his early years in the league, carried 252 pounds on a 6-foot-6-inch frame but was surprisingly quick. The 1993 MVP became only the second NBA player (after Wilt Chamberlain) to top 23,000 points, 12,000 rebounds, and 4,000 assists.

Karl Malone (*left*) epitomized the power forward. An intimidating 256 pounds of rippled muscle stacked 6 feet 9 inches high, he was a force from the time he entered the NBA in 1984, battling in the lane for points and rebounds. "The paint is where men are made," he said. "That's where I earn my living." He was the league MVP in 1997 and 1999, trailing only Abdul-Jabbar and Chamberlain in career scoring.

At age 13 Shaquille O'Neal stood 6 feet 6 and wore size 17 shoes. By the time he turned pro in 1992, he was 7 feet 1 and weighed more than 300 pounds (*right, top*). The powerful giant—who made the NBA All-Rookie first team along with 6-foot-10 shot blocker Alonzo Mourning (*right*)—had explosive strength. Said former All-Star center Bill Walton: "It's a raw power that you don't get from the weight room. It comes from deep in the soul."

Shaquille O'Neal overmasters Houston's Hakeem Olajuwon. During the 1990s, Shaq recorded rap music, acted in movies, and pitched soft drinks when he wasn't scoring or rebounding.

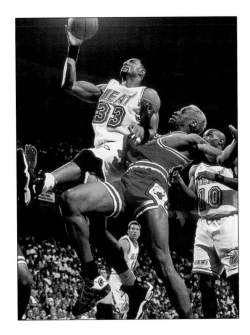

Alonzo Mourning outmuscles the colorful Dennis Rodman for a loose ball. A fierce on-court figure averaging 3.91 shot blocks per game, Mourning donated money to charity for each block.

Karl Malone powers over Chicago's Scottie Pippen in 1998. Malone, an 11-time All-Star with only 4.8 percent body fat, said, "Nobody ever stops me one-on-one."

Playmaking Geniuses

President John F. Kennedy was enough of a basketball fan to know greatness when he saw it. "The game bears an indelible stamp of your rare skills," he wired the Boston Celtics' Bob Cousy in 1963. The ultimate floor leader, Cousy controlled a game's tempo with his ball handling and dartlike passes—and point guards are still measured against him.

The first heirs to his crown were Oscar Robertson, Magic Johnson, and Isiah Thomas *(inset)*. The Big O averaged nearly 10 assists a game while finishing his career as one of the NBA's all-time leading scorers. Johnson, the quarterback of the fast-breaking Los Angeles Lakers, notched more assists than either Cousy or Robertson. And Thomas, a quick, clever playmaker, led the Detroit Pistons to two NBA crowns in the late 1980s. "I call him the baby-faced assassin," an opposing coach said of the 12-time All-Star, "because he smiles at you, then cuts you down."

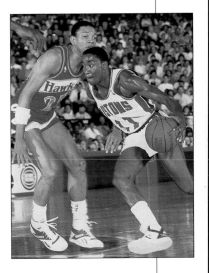

The best playmaker of all time, however, may have been John Stockton *(left)*. The Gonzaga graduate stood only 6 feet 1, but what he lacked in size he made up for with grit—missing only four games in his first 13 seasons—and heads-up play. Stockton broke Johnson's all-time assist record in 1995, topped 13,000 career assists in 1999, and showed no signs of stopping. Said teammate Karl Malone: "He's as steady as the ticktock of a clock."

Utah Jazz point guard John Stockton sends a backward pass safely out of the reach of Laker defenders during a 1998 play-off game.

The Glory That Was the Bulls

Scottie Pippen drives past Houston's Hakeem Olajuwon. "As long as he's playing with Michael [Jordan], Pippen is the second-best player in the league," said one writer. Pippen and Jordan played on all six Bulls championship teams.

No player has ever made basketball look as easy as Michael Jordan. Able to sink fadeaway jumpers as effortlessly as he could slash to the basket, hang in the air, and dunk, the agile 6-foot-6-inch guard was an obvious choice for Rookie of the Year in 1985. He landed a fat Nike shoe contract, and his shoe model was dubbed Air, which also became his nickname—for all the time he spent soaring through that medium. The following year he scored 63 points in a play-off game against the Boston Celtics. The performance set an NBA record and made Larry Bird think twice about whether Jordan was a mere mortal—"I think it's just God disguised as Michael Jordan," he said. But the Bulls still lost, in double overtime.

By the end of the decade, Jordan had parlayed his winning smile and almost supernatural talent into additional lucrative endorsements for everything from underwear to cereal. But he still had not won an NBA title. That would have to wait until after 1989, when Phil Jackson *(page 109)* became the Chicago coach. A minister's son and admirer of Zen Buddhism, the former New York Knick preached the virtues of teamwork and installed a half-court attack developed by assistant coach Tex Winter, called the triangle offense, that provided specific roles for Jordan's supporting cast.

Flying after a loose ball in a 1997 game against Golden State, Dennis Rodman gives a thumbs-up performance for courtside Bulls fans, including the late film critic Gene Siskel.

Scottie Pippen, John Paxson, Horace Grant, Bill Cartwright, and B. J. Armstrong all thrived under the system. Pippen, a wiry 6-foot-7-inch forward, blossomed into an All-Star, playing ferocious defense, handling the ball like a point guard, and hitting three-pointers. Led by Jordan, the Bulls beat the Los Angeles Lakers to become the 1991 champs. After winning 67 games and losing only 15 in the regular season, they brushed aside Portland for the 1992 crown as well, and the following year they won their third straight title. Meanwhile, year after year Jordan and his Bulls filled arenas wherever they played, grabbed huge TV ratings, boosted sales of team merchandise, and generally gave

Michael Jordan attacks. Said Utah coach Jerry Sloan: "Everybody knows how he should be remembered—as the greatest player ever."

the NBA such a financial lift that the well-being of the league virtually rested on His Airness's shoulders.

Then tragedy struck: Jordan's father was murdered, and Michael, saying he had lost his motivation, retired from basketball to try minor-league baseball instead. While he struggled to hit curve balls, the Bulls stumbled. Pippen elevated his game, but Chicago couldn't make it back to the Finals.

Jordan returned late in the 1994-95 campaign, and the following season the Bulls, who had acquired Croatian star Toni Kukoc, three-point specialist Steve Kerr, and ball hawk Dennis Rodman, were unstoppable once again. Kukoc, a versatile 6-foot-11-inch forward, added a spark off the bench. Rodman, a 6-foot-6-inch mass of tattoos, frequently made headlines with his dyed hair and wild off-court antics, but he was a prolific rebounder. They helped the Bulls to a league record 72 wins in 1996 and their fourth and fifth NBA crowns of the decade.

Jordan, pondering retirement as the Bulls tried in 1998 for their second "three-peat," wanted to say good-bye with flair. So in June, as the final seconds ticked off in game 6 of the championship series against Utah, he stole the ball and dribbled down the floor. Guarded closely, the five-time MVP and 10-time scoring leader cut right, stopped short, and took the final shot of his career *(right),* a 20-foot jumper that gave Chicago its sixth title in eight years. As the ball dropped through the hoop, Jordan stood motionless, his arm and hand extended in a perfect, lingering follow-through, for he had predicted the moment. "When I leave the game," he had written years before, "I'll leave on top."

The Hunt for an Air Apparent

Kobe Bryant, the youngest player ever to start in an NBA game, darts past an opponent.

Tim Duncan, shown flicking a pass to a teammate, was the 1997-98 Rookie of the Year.

Kevin Garnett slams the ball home as Patrick Ewing of the New York Knicks stands helpless.

When Michael Jordan announced his retirement in January 1999, two questions arose. The first—What's next for His Airness?—he answered himself: "I am just going to enjoy life and do some of the things I've never done before," he said, like picking up the kids after school. The second—What's next for the NBA?—was harder to answer. But as the game approached a new century, a posse of young stars stepped forward hoping to fill Jordan's Nikes.

Two of the most exciting were the Pistons' Grant Hill *(right)* and the Lakers' Kobe Bryant *(left, top)*. Hill was a star at Duke. Bryant jumped to the pros right from high school. Both had great genes: Hill was the son of former Dallas Cowboys star running back Calvin Hill; Bryant's father, Joe "Jellybean" Bryant, played eight seasons in the NBA. They shared deft ball handling and sweet shooting with Tim Duncan *(left)*. He led San Antonio to a title and became a contender for MVP honors—in just his second pro season.

Minnesota's Kevin Garnett *(left, bottom)*, only 19, also went from high school to the NBA. A year later he was an All-Star, and at 21 he was the highest-paid team-sport athlete ever, making $21 million a year. Philadelphia's Allen Iverson made his big leap after two years at Georgetown University. The owner of a lightning-quick crossover dribble *(inset)*, he scored 26.8 points a game and won the 1998-99 scoring title. Said an NBA team president: "You can't guard him." It's just what they used to say about Jordan.

Allen Iverson drives for two. He was the first 'Sixer since Chamberlain to lead the NBA in scoring.

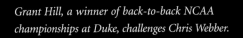

*Grant Hill, a winner of back-to-back NCAA
championships at Duke, challenges Chris Webber.*

Speed for Sport's Sake

★

THE FIERCE JOY OF GOING FASTEST

In 776 BC Koroibos of Elis triumphed at the first Olympics. He outpaced all challengers at the Games' single event, a 200-yard footrace. Almost 2,800 years later speed remains at the heart of athletic competition, and those who prove the swiftest—whether on foot, in water, or, like A. J. Foyt *(inset)*, piloting a missile on wheels—still find a lasting place in sports legend.

There is perhaps no more basic expression of the human capacity for speed than running, straining every muscle to power one's way past competitors toward the laurel wreath of victory. And in the long line of brilliant American runners, Michael Johnson staked out a special niche. Johnson excelled in two events that are normally considered mutually exclusive—the 200-meter dash and the 400-meter run. The 200 calls for pure speed, the 400 for endurance. Johnson proved he had both, in 1995 becoming the first man ever to win both events in international competition, at the track-and-field World Championships. He repeated the feat at the Olympics the following year. Toeing the line for the Olympic 200 in a pair of custom-made golden shoes *(left)*, he stumbled at the start, recovered, and zoomed

At the 1996 Olympics, Michael Johnson blazes to victory in the 200 meters, running in his distinctive upright style. "He's like a statue," said his high-school coach. "They say his feet never leave the ground."

Carl Lewis rounds a curve on his way to winning the 200-meter dash by the largest margin in Olympic history in 1984 at Los Angeles. He set a world record in the event at the '88 Games.

to the tape in an astonishing 19.32 seconds, shattering his own record. At the 1999 World Championships Johnson ran the 400 in a best-ever time of 43.18 seconds. He also came away with the ninth world championship gold medal of his career, eclipsing Carl Lewis's eight.

Lewis was the superstar sprinter of the 1980s and early 1990s, reigning for more than a decade as the fastest man on earth. At the 1984 Olympics he won the 100 meters—registering a jaw-dropping 28 miles per hour at the finish—and then triumphed in the long jump, the 200 meters *(left)*, and the 4 x 100-meter relay, duplicating with these four victories Jesse Owens's legendary 1936 performance *(page 166)*. When his father died in 1987, Lewis placed his 100-meter gold medal in the coffin, saying, "I want you to have this because it was your favorite event." Then, seeing his grieving mother's surprise, he said, "Don't worry, I'll get another one." Lewis went on to set a new world record for the 100 meters in 1991 and to run his Olympic gold medal total to nine by 1996.

Like Lewis before her, Gail Devers enjoyed repeat Olympic victories in the 100 meters *(left, bottom)*, overcoming terrifying hardships to regain her dazzling power and form *(page 70)*. But as fast as Devers ran in the 1992 and 1996 Olympics, the swiftest woman of all time remained the scintillating Florence Griffith-Joyner *(right)*—known to friends and fans simply as FloJo. Adding world-class glamour and beauty to unimaginable speed, Griffith-Joyner became celebrated for her flowing hair, elaborately painted nails, and often spectacular track attire. At the 1988 U.S. Olympic trials her world-record time in the 100-meter dash surpassed the men's record in several countries. It was no surprise when she took the gold in that event at the Seoul Olympics, but her historic time in the 200 meters prompted the astonished silver medalist, Grace Jackson of Jamaica, to declare, "It's out of reach for us."

Griffith-Joyner's life proved to be as brilliant and brief as her races: She died of a seizure in 1998 at the age of 38, her record times in the 100 and 200 meters still unsurpassed.

American Gail Devers (right) beats out Merlene Ottey of Jamaica (left) to win the 100-meter dash at the 1996 Olympic Games in Atlanta—by a margin of only five thousandths of a second.

Florence Griffith-Joyner flashes to a new world record in the 200-meter semifinals at the 1988 Seoul Olympics. She then broke that record while winning the final.

Eric Heiden displays the awesome power he would use in sweeping all five speed skating events at the 1980 Olympics. Heiden set one world record and four Olympic records at the Games.

Fire on Ice
and Snow

Speed skating receives little attention in the United States. Thus Wisconsin teenager Eric Heiden labored in anonymity as he trained to develop strength and technique. He placed 10th, as a 17-year-old, in his first international meet in 1975. At the Innsbruck Olympics a year later he finished seventh and 19th in his two events. Those were the last speed skating races he would ever lose.

When he took the 1977, '78, and '79 World Championships, skating-mad Scandinavia cheered. But it was only at the 1980 Olympics in Lake Placid, New York, that the modest young man caught his own country's attention. Like runners, speed skaters specialize in either sprints or distance races. Heiden acknowledged no such limits. With blades slashing, arms whipping, and massive thighs pumping, he overwhelmed his sport, becoming the first man to sweep all five Olympic speed skating events, from 500 to 10,000 meters. Awed by his versatility, Norwegian coach Sten Stenson said, "It's like having the best sprinter in the world entering the marathon and winning it."

The quiet life was not Picabo (pronounced PEEK-a-boo) Street's style. With a personality as vivid as her auburn ponytail, Street grew up in tiny Triumph, Idaho, and started skiing at age five. A downhill skier can go as fast as nerve and the laws of physics allow, sometimes exceeding 80 miles an hour. The fearless Street arrived on the world scene with an Olympic silver medal in 1994. She then scooped up two World Cup downhill titles. But in a 1996 crash she tore up her left knee, recovering only to suffer a concussion in another spill just days before she left for the 1998 Olympics in Nagano, Japan.

Nonetheless, Street declared herself in "tiger mode." Gold eluded her again in the downhill at Nagano, but she unexpectedly sped to victory through the twists and turns of the super-giant slalom *(inset)*. "Since I was 10 I wanted a gold medal," she said cheerfully. "I got it."

> ## "I didn't get into skating to be famous. . . . If I wanted to be famous, I would have stuck with hockey."
>
> Eric Heiden

Picabo Street charges through the super-giant slalom course at the 1998 Winter Olympics in Nagano, Japan. As the race began, she told herself, "It's gold time. Let's go!" Her gold medal marked the first time she had ever won that event in international competition.

Mark Spitz's mustache shows his confidence at the 1972 Olympics; most swimmers shave clean to cut down resistance. Spitz came to Munich with much to prove: He had, as a highly rated and cocky U.S. prospect, failed to win an individual event at the 1968 Games.

"Size doesn't matter as long as you can get to the end of the pool faster than anybody else."

Janet Evans

Janet Evans propels herself into the pool at the start of the 400-meter freestyle at the 1988 Olympic Games in Seoul. The slender high-school student powered her way past heftier competitors to take a gold medal in the event—and beat her own world-record time.

Smoke on the Water

The late 19th century saw a rebirth of the ancient sport of competitive swimming, as well as the development of the modern freestyle stroke. Since that time America has produced a long line of legendary swimmers. One of the earliest stars of the pool was Duke Kahanamoku, the grandson of a Hawaiian high chief. Kahanamoku seized the world's attention at the 1912 Olympics, where he won the 100-meter freestyle, the first of his three Olympic gold medals. Later he became known as the father of modern surfing, a sport once reserved for Hawaiian royalty.

Johnny Weissmuller succeeded Kahanamoku as America's top swimmer. The son of an immigrant coal miner, he began setting new world records while still a teenager and won a total of five gold medals in the 1924 and 1928 Olympics. He went through his entire amateur swimming career without ever losing a race, and this perfect record, combined with his charm, raised swimming to new popularity. In 1932 Weissmuller traded his swim trunks for a loincloth to star in the first of a dozen Tarzan movies.

Matt Biondi *(right)* and Janet Evans *(left, bottom)*, swimming stars of the 1988 Olympics in Seoul, were a study in contrasts. Biondi stood 6 feet 6 and weighed 200 pounds; Evans was a foot shorter and barely made 100 pounds. Biondi had a textbook freestyle stroke; Evans swam with a rapid straight-armed style all her own. But they matched each other in success. Evans, just 17 and the darling of the Games, captured three gold medals, and Biondi took home five.

Biondi and Evans shone at Seoul, but the most brilliant swimming star of all time remained Mark Spitz *(left, top)*. At the 1972 Olympics, Spitz competed in four individual and three team events—and took a gold medal in each. Never before had an athlete won seven golds in a single Olympics. To make his feat even more breathtaking, every win was accomplished in world-record time.

Matt Biondi, surging through the water in Seoul, earned 11 swimming medals in three Olympics, a record he shared with Mark Spitz.

The Finest of the Breed

Talk of the greatest American horses almost always begins with Man o' War, who was a national hero in the 1920s. Antigambling sentiment had badly damaged horse racing in the years before the enormous chestnut colt made his winning debut in 1919. "Big Red" so thrilled spectators that he not only reestablished the sport's popularity but turned the United States into the racing center of the world. Running in huge bounds, Man o' War set one speed record after another. In his two years of competition, he won 20 out of 21 races, taking one of them by an incredible 100 lengths. He was, one sportswriter declared, "a living flame."

Man o' War's status as the greatest of the century remained unchallenged for two decades. Then, in 1947, a bay colt from Maryland named Citation launched a four-year career that made him a competitor for that title. Citation became racing's eighth Triple Crown winner in 1948, taking the Kentucky Derby, the Preakness, and the Belmont Stakes by a combined 17 lengths. Impressive as these victories were, they made up only part of an incredible 15-race winning streak—one of them a rare walkover, a race in which no other horse was entered.

Citation's stature grew as the next 25 years failed to produce another Triple Crown winner. Then Secretariat entered the scene. In 1972 he was named Horse of the Year, an unusual honor for a two-year-old, and expectations ran high for his 1973 season. Nicknamed Big Red like the legendary Man o' War, he surpassed onlookers' wildest dreams.

Secretariat started his Triple Crown bid with a display of speed that has been called the finest Kentucky Derby run ever: He came from the back of the pack to win in record time *(right)*. The Preakness brought another win and another stunning run.

But the best came last. At the Belmont—that mile-and-a-half conqueror of many a Triple Crown hopeful—Secretariat just kept gaining speed, finishing an incredible 31 lengths ahead of the rest of the field in record-shattering time. Veteran horsemen watching the race were horrified, believing that jockey Ron Turcotte was unaccountably driving the horse to certain destruction. But Secretariat had simply romped. "I know this sounds crazy," Turcotte later said, "but the horse did it by himself. I was along for the ride." It was a peerless performance that left commentators at a loss for comparisons. As Charles Hatton of the *Daily Racing Form* said, "His only point of reference is himself."

His hooves thundering and the dirt flying, mighty Secretariat opens his assault on the Triple Crown by breaking clear and heading to the wire in the 1973 Kentucky Derby.

Jeff Gordon heats up the track—and the NASCAR Winston Cup circuit. The sport's young superstar amassed $26 million in earnings between 1992 and 1998.

From Dirt Tracks to Superspeedways

Speed in sport occurs at its utmost in auto racing. Whether the competition is Indy Car, Formula One, or the National Association for Stock Car Auto Racing (NASCAR), the drivers must master blinding speed, their own nerves, crushing g-forces, and cockpit temperatures that approach 140 degrees.

Versatility was the hallmark of Mario Andretti in a career that lasted from the 1950s to the '90s. He won the two signature American races, the Indy 500 and NASCAR's Daytona 500, and in 1978 was Formula One champion. Texan A. J. Foyt was an Indy Car fixture for 35 years. Strapped into a horizontal tube, just inches above a pavement whipping past at well over 200 miles per hour, Foyt became the first four-time winner of the Indianapolis 500. But he also racked up seven victories in NASCAR's top racing class—the Grand National (later Winston Cup) series.

NASCAR started as a rebel's circuit, where moonshiners' sons, driving cars souped up in their backyards, met on dirt tracks to test the driving skills they had learned evading federal revenue agents while hauling loads of "corn squeezins" on Appalachian back roads. But it was Richard Petty of North Carolina who brought stock-car racing to the masses, with its full-throttle "drafting"—nose-to-tail driving for aerodynamic boost—as well as the bumping and grinding through tight turns by hard-charging drivers. Petty earned fans nationwide with a record 200 NASCAR wins.

By the late 1990s Winston Cup racing was the nation's fastest-growing sport, and its star was a soft-spoken young Californian named Jeff Gordon. He became Rookie of the Year in 1993 and champion driver three of the next five years. Piloting a Chevrolet Monte Carlo *(left)* that looked little like showroom models, Gordon fed the appetite of a growing segment of fans for that hallmark of sport—all-out speed.

The Gridiron
Game

★

A CENTURY OF HARD KNOCKS AND GLORY

Over the course of the century football has evolved toward increasing complexity: intricate offenses and defenses, special teams, hordes of assistant coaches. Yet at bottom the game is about hitting. From Jim Thorpe's days with the Canton (Ohio) Bulldogs *(inset)* to the modern era of the New York Giants' Lawrence Taylor *(right)*, players and fans alike have been drawn to football's dramatic spectacle of choreographed violence.

In Thorpe's time the Ivy League was the focus of action. His college team, Carlisle Indian School, coached by Hall of Famer Glenn "Pop" Warner, lacked high academic standing but often schooled the scholar-athletes of Yale and Columbia. The college game was brutal: In 1905 18 young men died playing. Harvard was the sport's standout, losing just once from November 1911 until 1915. The defeat, 18-5, was at Carlisle's hands, as Thorpe drop-kicked or ran in every point.

After the Ivy League's early run, supremacy in college football shifted to the Midwest, where the young professional game was also active. Pro teams in big cities played against small-town outfits like the Rock Island (Illinois) Independents and Thorpe's Bulldogs. Free agency was rampant. "A guy would be on your team one week and playing against you the next," remembered Chicago Bears owner and coach George Halas. "Ask him why and he'd say, 'Because they offered me five dollars more.' "

New York Giants outside linebacker Lawrence Taylor flattens Dallas Cowboys quarterback Gary Hogeboom in a 1985 game. The 237-pound Hall of Famer meted out 130 sacks during his 13 years on the field.

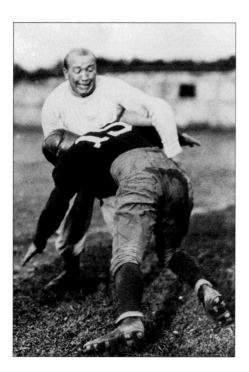

Renowned Notre Dame coach Knute Rockne, a former pro end, practices tackles with one of the Fighting Irish he drove to a 13-season record of 105-12-5.

"The Four Horsemen rode again," wrote columnist Grantland Rice—not those of the Apocalypse, but of Notre Dame: from left, Don Miller, Elmer Layden, Jim Crowley, Harry Stuhldreher.

These squads were incorporated in 1920 in the American Professional Football Association (renamed two years later the National Football League), with Jim Thorpe, still playing for Canton, serving as figurehead president. One of the small-town entries was the Green Bay Packers, sponsored by a local meat packing firm. Today Green Bay is the NFL's sole small-town survivor, recalling the pro game's rough-and-ready beginnings while sharing in its current big-buck, media-saturated glitz. Only the hitting remains the same.

Gridiron Heartland. In the NFL's early years "real" football was viewed as a rough but clean sport for rough but clean college boys, and playing for pay was somewhat disreputable. The center of gravity for the game remained the collegiate Midwest, whose Western Conference, later popularly known as the Big Ten, continually produced powerhouse teams like Michigan, Illinois, and Ohio State.

Illinois's Harold E. "Red" Grange was football's Dempsey, Tilden, and Ruth. Writer Damon Runyon once said of him, "On the field, he is the equal of three men and a horse." In a 1924 Illinois-Michigan clash, Grange racked up four touchdowns in 12 minutes. Playing to huge crowds and breathless newspaper headlines, he tore off slithering runs in which he was as hard to tackle as a phantasm, earning him the nickname Galloping Ghost.

In 1925 Grange *(right)* signed on with Halas's Bears, who then went on a nationwide barnstorming tour with a killer schedule—eight games in 12 days, followed by a month-long odyssey to the Deep South and West Coast. As in college, Grange drew mobs of fans wherever he played, single-handedly giving the NFL legitimacy.

The preeminent college team was Notre Dame. Coach Knute Rockne *(left, top)* had starred there himself, hooking up on the field with his roommate, quarterback Gus Dorais, to turn the little-used forward pass into a prolific offensive weapon. As coach of the Fighting Irish, Rockne assembled and trained a backfield *(left)* so formidable that sportswriter Grantland Rice used an apocalyptic biblical reference to characterize their destructive effect on opposing teams: "Outlined against a blue-gray October sky, the

Red Grange (far right) huddles with Chicago teammates, all disciples of George "Papa Bear" Halas, the pro game's longest-serving coach.

Two-way star Sammy Baugh, Washington Redskins quarterback from 1937 to 1952, led the NFL not just in passes but also in punts and interceptions.

Four Horsemen rode again." One of Rockne's players, it turned out, had an ear for the memorable phrase himself. When George Gipp, a brilliant halfback, lay dying of pneumonia, he told his coach, "Someday in a tough game, ask the players to win one for the Gipper." Between 1919 and 1930 Rockne's Irish experienced few tough games, going undefeated five times.

But the honor of the best single season of all time went to the 1939 University of Tennessee, which outscored opponents 212 to 0 (*right*). What's more, that perfect 10-0-0 season was only the center cut of a string of 17 consecutive regular-season games between 1938 and 1940 in which the Volunteers held their opponents scoreless. Ironically, Tennessee, temporarily brought low by key injuries, was itself shut out 14-0 by Southern California in the Rose Bowl game following the 1939 season.

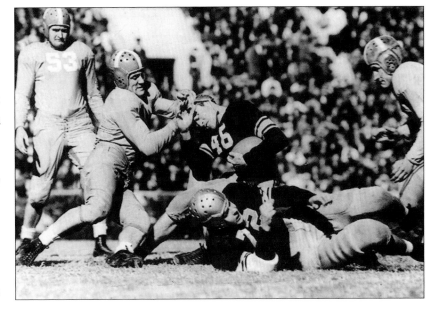

Tough Tennessee linebacker Len Coffman rips the helmet from LSU halfback Charles Anastasio but leaves the head. The Vols won the game 20-0 in 1939, the year no one scored against them.

Made for Each Other. The first televised football game occurred on October 22, 1939, at Ebbets Field, between the NFL's Brooklyn Dodgers and Philadelphia Eagles. The 13,000 spectators in the stands far outnumbered NBC's tiny New York City audience of pioneer couch potatoes, who squinted at snow-flecked images on midget screens that grew darker as the day wore on. No player knew he was making history, but even then it was clear to a few visionaries that football and TV were a perfect match.

"Football by television invites audience participation," wrote Orrin E. Dunlap Jr., covering the event for the *New York Times*. "The spectator at the gridiron does not have that intimacy with the players; he knows the game is separate from him because he is sandwiched in the crowd; the gladiators are out on the field. But by television the contest is in the living room; the spectator is edged up close."

The future that Dunlap foresaw in 1939 was more than a decade away, but the game did not wait. Standout players like "Slinging Sammy" Baugh (*left*), the pinpoint-passing field general of the Washington Redskins, inspired fans' imagination. And a social revolution took place. Many blacks had played in pro football's early days, but from 1933 to 1946 an unspoken rule had kept them out of the NFL. Then, beating Jackie Robinson's entry into Major League Baseball by a year, the Los Angeles Rams signed

L.A. Rams halfback Kenny Washington slips past a tackler. An All-American at UCLA, Washington in 1946 became the first black player signed by an NFL franchise in more than a decade.

An official signals touchdown after Baltimore Colt Alan Ameche's plunge into the Giants' end zone in sudden-death overtime to wrap up "the greatest game ever played." One of the first nationally televised games, the December 1958 thriller showcased the Colts' immortal quarterback Johnny Unitas (below).

college stars Kenny Washington *(page 143)* and Woody Strode.

By the mid-1950s, football officials and network and advertising executives fully appreciated the symmetry between the new TV medium and the rules and compact alignment of the game. The backfield and offensive and defensive lines fit neatly on the screen. And the time-outs and breaks between halves and quarters were natural niches for commercials. Fans now numbered in the millions. No longer simply a game, football was rapidly becoming a powerful marketing tool.

A Revolution in the Game. In 1946 the All-America Football Conference (AAFC) opened for business to challenge the NFL. Dominating the new league from the start was the Cleveland Browns, who won the championship all four years of the AAFC's existence. Four teams disappeared when the NFL absorbed the three strongest AAFC members after the 1949 season. Just two—the San Francisco 49ers and the Browns—survived.

Cleveland's team was the creation of Paul Brown, its autocratic and wildly successful coach. Brown's innovations included playbooks, a fulltime coaching staff, play-calling from the sidelines, and spotters in the stands. The Browns, greeted with contempt by the established teams, were matched against the defending champion Philadelphia Eagles in their NFL inaugural game in 1950. They proceeded to drub the Eagles and, over the next six years, add six consecutive division titles and three league championships to their four from the AAFC.

After Cleveland's memorable skein, two other teams met in a championship game for the ages. On December 28, 1958, before 64,000-plus spectators and millions more watching on TV, the Giants battled the Baltimore Colts. The Colts' great quarterback, John Unitas *(left),* led them to a 14-3 halftime lead. A catch by halfback Frank Gifford from Charley Conerly moved the Giants ahead in the fourth quarter. Unitas quickly drove Baltimore back up the field, and Steve Myhra kicked a field goal to tie the game, setting up a situation that had fans wonderstruck—the NFL's first-ever sudden-death overtime. The Giants received but were unable to move the ball and punted. Then Unitas deftly alternated passes and runs, ending with running back Alan Ameche's dive to victory from the one-yard line *(left, top).* "The greatest game ever played," fans and sportswriters agreed.

After faltering for a year, the Browns returned to the NFL's elite on the shoulders of another Brown, their new running back named Jim *(right).* In nine seasons the 6-foot-2-inch, 230-pound fullback defined the ground

Cleveland's nonpareil running back Jim Brown hammers through a mud-slick 49ers defense at San Francisco's Kezar Stadium in December 1962.

After a vicious hit in 1960, Philadelphia Eagles linebacker Chuck Bednarik looms triumphantly over New York Giants halfback Frank Gifford, unconscious and badly concussed.

Giants quarterback Y. A. Tittle, 37, kneels like a shell-shocked soldier in his own end zone after a brutal sack by Steelers lineman John Baker in a 1964 game at Pittsburgh.

game, *averaging* 104 yards per contest—12,312 in all. Bigger than many linemen, Brown was powerful enough to run over defenders, fast enough to charge past them, and elusive enough to juke them out of their shoes. "All you can do," observed Giants linebacker Sam Huff—who did it best —"is grab him, hold on, and wait for help."

A Flowering of Focused Mayhem. In the 1960s TV's close-in shots and slow-motion replays spotlighted the game's violence. Gnarled old-school defensive backs like the Eagles' Chuck Bednarik *(left)* made almost a fetish of hitting hard, and courageous but vulnerable offensive backs like Y. A. Tittle of the Giants *(left, bottom)* often paid the price. At the summit of pain-inflicting toughness was middle linebacker Dick Butkus *(right, top),* who joined the Bears in 1965. In one tackle he shattered a runner's face mask with his own. "If I had a choice," said an opposing ball carrier, "I'd sooner go one-on-one with a grizzly bear. I prayed that I could get up every time Butkus hit me." The 6-foot-3-inch, 245-pound Butkus had the strength to tackle a runner with one arm while stripping him of the ball with the other, setting a record for career fumble recoveries. To attain mental preparedness for such marauding, he once said, "I would manufacture things to make me mad. If someone on the other team was laughing, I'd pretend he was laughing at me or the Bears."

Butkus's equal in linebacking fury was Ray Nitschke *(near right)* of the Packers. Although he did not, as rumored, eat barbed wire, the bald-pated Nitschke did tightly tape his arms to mask injuries—and to better stun runners with forearm blows. While Nitschke and Butkus rumbled in midfield, a fellow assassin in the NFL's Central "Black-and-Blue" Division was Detroit defensive lineman Alex Karras *(far right),* who mauled opposing blockers and the quarterbacks and runners they were supposed to protect with equal glee.

Thanks to the popularity of this rock 'em-sock 'em game, money was pouring into the NFL owners' coffers. Businessmen on the outside wanted to cut themselves in, and they did so in 1960 by establishing the American Football League (AFL). From the start the prevailing style of play in the AFL was a crowd-pleasing brand of high-flying, high-scoring offense; defense was seldom to be seen. The new league won a network TV contract, and despite an expensive salary war with the NFL, by 1964 all the AFL's teams were operating in the black.

After years of mutual insults and costly competition for players, the two leagues finally sat down together in 1966 and agreed on a merger—to be completed in 1970, with the AFL becoming the American Football Conference

Chicago middle linebacker Dick Butkus terrorized NFL quarterbacks for nine years before knee injuries sidelined the affable but ferocious grizzly of the Bears.

Expressing perpetual rage, Green Bay linebacker and feared pass interceptor Ray Nitschke roars at the Bears' offensive line.

Detroit defensive tackle Alex Karras, leader of the Lions' "Fearsome Foursome," vaults fallen Giants blockers in 1964.

Shielded from the sun by his trademark hound's-tooth check hat, Paul "Bear" Bryant commands his Alabama Crimson Tide toward one more victory for the winningest coach in NCAA I-A ball.

A disheveled Woody Hayes makes himself heard as he strides off the field after Ohio State's 1962 defeat of Iowa State. Even in victory Hayes was as aggressive as a linebacker.

(AFC) and the NFL becoming the NFC. The first step on the road to the merger would be a championship game in January 1967, Super Bowl I.

College Football's Staying Power. In the decades pro football spent searching for commercial success, college teams prospered from generous alumni and sold-out stadiums, and a number of coaches became famous for their winning programs. Bob Neyland coached the Tennessee Volunteers from 1926 to 1952—with a few interruptions for military service—registering a 173-31-12 record, including the "perfect" 1939 season *(page 143)*. From 1941 through 1953 Frank Leahy led Notre Dame to six unbeaten seasons, retiring with a winning percentage of .864. Bud Wilkinson's Oklahoma Sooners ran off an NCAA record 47 straight wins between 1953 and 1957.

Two coaches stood out not only for the success of their teams but also for their colorful personalities. Paul "Bear" Bryant *(left)* got his nickname because he'd once wrestled one to win a precious five dollars during hard times. He was big and fast enough to get an athletic scholarship to Alabama. His first head coaching job was at Maryland, followed by Kentucky, which he molded into a championship team, then Texas A&M, and more championships. But in 1958 he said, "Mama's calling," and he went "home" to Alabama.

Bryant had a reputation as a hard taskmaster, and he was preceded at Alabama by stories about the rigorous training camp he had run at A&M: One tale said the camp was so strenuous the players went there in two buses and came back in one. He quickly turned a losing Crimson Tide program into a perennial winner. By the time he retired in 1982, he had amassed more victories than any other college coach: 323 against 85 losses. Bryant was so bound to football he evidently could not live without it. A few months after his retirement he succumbed to a heart attack.

Wayne Woodrow "Woody" Hayes *(left)* grew up and spent his career in Ohio, coaching at Denison and Miami of Ohio before signing on at an institution that had become known as the graveyard of coaches. Ohio State fans, unwilling to accept less than the return of Paul Brown, who had coached OSU for three seasons a decade earlier, hounded several coaches out of Columbus. Hayes put an end to all that. His commanding leadership of the Buckeyes, beginning in 1951, brought results: 13 Big Ten crowns; eight Rose Bowl appearances, including four in a row; four unbeaten seasons; and five with just one loss. Often chided for heavy reliance on the running game,

Bathed in California sunlight, peerless USC running back O. J. Simpson walks away from college football after his final game, following the money to Buffalo.

Braving below-zero temperatures in 1967, more than 50,000 Green Bay fans watched Packer quarterback Bart Starr defeat Dallas 21-17 with a quarterback sneak in the final seconds of play.

Vince Lombardi trains his Packers with a chalkboard lecture, using techniques he'd once applied in teaching high-school Latin to build a team that was as smart as it was strong.

he retorted, "Three things can happen when you pass, and two of them are bad." Hayes's dynamic reign ended abruptly in 1978 when he was forced to retire after his famous temper got the better of him and he punched an opposing player who had intercepted a Buckeye pass in a bowl game.

College football continued to serve as a nursery for the upbringing of future pros. One of the best and most famous was running back O. J. Simpson *(page 149)* of Southern California. His broken-field agility left tacklers grasping at air, and his power and stamina wore out defensive lines. At USC he won the Heisman Trophy and a national title; drafted by the Buffalo Bills in 1969, he gained a record 273 yards in a game and more than 2,000 in a season.

Big Time in a Small Town. By the late 1950s the once great Green Bay Packers had devolved to one of the NFL's worst teams. To revive them Packers management hired 45-year-old New Yorker Vince Lombardi *(below)*, then a Giants assistant coach. Lombardi had the confidence of a rhino, fortified with the orderly mind of an ex-Latin teacher. "Gentlemen," he told his new charges, "I've never been associated with a losing team. I do not intend to start now."

Lombardi wasn't joking. He drilled blockers as he had drilled students on Latin clauses, making his players do everything again and again and again. Players who fumbled had to take showers with the football. Under his tutelage, a middling quarterback named Bart Starr grew into one of the NFL's best, promising acquisitions like Paul Hornung and Jim Taylor delivered thumping runs, and Willie Davis and Herb Adderley smothered opposing offenses. The toughness he drilled into his team showed in the famous 1967 "Ice Bowl" *(left, top)* in Green Bay, when the Packers played without gloves in minus-13-degree weather and beat the Dallas Cowboys for the NFL championship. As long as Lombardi held sway, the Pack was formidable. They won five NFL titles and dominated the first two Super Bowls.

Then Lombardi announced his retirement, and the powerful Baltimore Colts arose to represent the NFL in Super Bowl III. Virtually everyone

"Broadway Joe" Namath, the New York Jets' brash quarterback, looks for a receiver during Super Bowl III. He validated his boast to defeat the highly favored Baltimore Colts and led the Jets to the AFL's first Super Bowl crown.

Miami's Larry Csonka bulls his way through a tangle of fallen Redskins, as the Dolphins register their first Super Bowl victory by a 14-7 score to complete a perfect season.

The Raiders' ancient George Blanda kicks one of his four field goals in Oakland's 40-7 win over the Houston Oilers for the 1967 AFL title.

expected them to continue the older league's supremacy against a lightly regarded champion—the New York Jets—of the lightly regarded AFL. The opposing teams' quarterbacks were a study in contrasts: Colts QBs Johnny Unitas and Earl Morrall were proud blue-collar crew-cut types who played in no-nonsense black shoes. The Jets' "Broadway Joe" Namath *(page 151)* brandished white shoes, long hair, and a Fu Manchu mustache. Said the playboy from Beaver Falls, Pennsylvania: "I like my Johnnie Walker Red and my women blonde." Before the big game Namath made headlines by stating, "We're going to win Sunday. I'll guarantee you." To the shock of NFL partisans, he backed up his boast, completing 17 of 28 passes in a 16-7 triumph.

A Trio of Champions. Succeeding seasons would prove that Namath's victory was no fluke, as three AFC teams won nine of the 12 Super Bowls from 1973 through 1984. From the early 1960s to the mid-1980s the Oakland Raiders were a brawling, much penalized but talented team. At quarterback they had natural athlete Daryle Lamonica, succeeded by the hard-nosed Ken "the Snake" Stabler. Al Davis was the cool, calculating owner, John Madden the manic coach. Seasoning the Raiders' stew of young stars was place-kicker and backup quarterback George Blanda *(left, bottom),* the oldest player in NFL history and the league's all-time leading scorer, who finally hung up his cleats at age 48. Except for their 1968 loss to Green Bay, the Raiders won all their Super Bowls—in 1977, 1981, and (now in L.A.) 1984.

The '70s saw the sudden rise of the Miami Dolphins, who in 1970 came under the control of former Baltimore coach Don Shula. The following season they made it to Super Bowl VI, losing 24-3 to Tom Landry's Dallas Cowboys, a football machine featuring quarterback Roger Staubach and defensive terror Bob Lilly. That was the last time the Dolphins would lose for a while. They swept through the '72 season, the play-offs, and the Super Bowl, posting an NFL record 17-0-0 season. Winning the Super Bowl again in '74, Miami might have rolled through the rest of the decade, propelled by Bob Griese at quarterback, wide receiver Paul Warfield, a backfield with stolid Larry Csonka *(left, top)* and Jim Kiick, and their No-Name Defense. But the 1974 start-up of the short-lived World Football League stole away Csonka, Kiick, and Warfield, leaving holes not even Shula could make good.

The revitalized Pittsburgh Steelers of the 1970s rode on four main rails: clockwise from top left, running back Franco Harris, quarterback Terry Bradshaw, wide receiver Lynn Swann, and tackle "Mean" Joe Greene, part of Pittsburgh's dreaded Steel Curtain defensive team.

Boston College's Doug Flutie is shown releasing his 48-yard, last-second "Hail Mary" pass to beat Miami of Florida in 1984.

Coaching for much of his 57-year career in the South of Jim Crow policies and attitudes, Eddie Robinson worked miracles in making Grambling into a perennial football power and turning out players like Super Bowl MVP Doug Williams.

The Pittsburgh Steelers, coached by Chuck Noll, built up weapons like a nation preparing for war *(page 153)*. In 1970 they found an unpolished gem in quarterback Terry Bradshaw from little Louisiana Tech. Carefully scouting black colleges, they discovered defensive tackle "Mean" Joe Greene and receiver John Stallworth. In 1972 they added running back Franco Harris, then glue-fingered pass catcher Lynn Swann and pile-driving linebacker Jack Lambert. Greene, who surely knew, said, "Jack Lambert is so mean he doesn't even like himself." The dominating team of the '70s, the Steelers went undefeated in four Super Bowls, beating the Minnesota Vikings, Dallas twice, and the Rams.

The Heart of the Offense. After a brilliant collegiate career at Notre Dame, Joe Montana *(right)* was drafted by the San Francisco 49ers, whose brainy coach, Bill Walsh, later said: "When Joe was in synch, he had an intuitive, instinctive nature rarely equaled by any athlete in any sport." In 1982 the 13-1 49ers stole the National Football Conference championship from Dallas with "the Catch"—Dwight Clark's last-minute, leaping, fingertip reception of a Montana pass in the end zone. In Super Bowl XVI two weeks later they beat

the Cincinnati Bengals 26-21. Then in the 1985 game they trampled the Dolphins 38-16. In 1989 they overcame the Bengals again, and the next year added to Denver's Super Bowl woes, 55-10. When Montana retired in 1995 many hailed him as the best quarterback ever.

Perhaps the best play ever belonged to Doug Flutie *(left, top)*, Boston College's diminutive QB. In a 1984 slugfest with defending national champ Miami, Flutie's team trailed 45-41 with six seconds left. The 5-foot-9-inch quarterback hurled a prayer of a pass —a kind known thereafter as a Hail Mary. His roommate Gerard Phelan went up amid a swarm of defenders and somehow came down with the ball and fell into the end zone for the win. Another author of a quarterback milestone was Doug Williams *(inset)* of the Redskins, who in 1988 became the first African American QB to

Arguably the greatest quarterback in football history, San Francisco's Joe Montana scrambles to avoid rushing defenders while, with a preternatural poise, he looks downfield for a receiver in red.

lead his team to a Super Bowl championship, with a 42-10 trouncing of Denver. Williams set a record with four touchdown passes—all in the 'Skins' 35-point second quarter—and broke Joe Montana's Super Bowl yardage record, winning MVP honors for the game.

Williams had been a protégé of Eddie Robinson (*page 154, bottom left*) of all-black Grambling State University, the winningest coach in college history. During his 57-year reign Robinson made a big social statement in piling up a record 408 wins at the chronically under-funded Louisiana school and sending more than 200 players on to the NFL. "He'd cry before a big game," recalled Williams, who later returned to his Grambling roots to take over as coach after Robinson retired.

The Running Game. Size and strength do not begin to describe the qualities of good ball carriers. "They also have to enjoy the chase," said Larry Csonka, who pounded through linemen for 6,737 yards in his eight years with the Dolphins. "If you were a kid who loved to have people chase you, you've got the beginnings of a running back."

Cleveland's Jim Brown and Chicago's Gale Sayers were the 1960s' model runners. The 1970s had Franco Harris, whose career would embrace almost seven miles of rushing yards. In the 1980s the men of the Redskins offensive line, who proudly called themselves the Hogs, named rugged John Riggins (*right, top*) an honorary Hog, because, said one, "he likes to get down in the mud." The best single-season performance by a ball carrier was turned in by the Rams' Eric Dickerson (*right*), who in 1984 rushed for 2,105 yards.

The most versatile was one of the smallest, Walter Payton (*left*). A granitic yet lithe 5-foot-10-inch 202-pounder, he had marvelous acceleration, hands that attracted thrown footballs, and a willingness to hit, to hurdle, and sometimes, it seemed, to levitate. He burrowed through defenders like a raging mole. "I want to go up the middle," he declared, "hit one guy, bounce off, hit another and another, jump over someone and fight for the extra yard. I don't want to just break free around end and run unobstructed."

In 13 seasons with the Bears Payton missed only one game, and that on an assistant coach's whim. He ignored injuries. By the end of his final season

The Bears' Walter Payton, going against "Black-and-Blue" Division rival the Detroit Lions, displays his usual gravity-defying grace during a 1984 game.

In a famous Super Bowl moment, Redskin John Riggins is slowed but not stopped by Dolphins defender Don McNeal in 1983. Riggins broke free for a 43-yard TD run as Washington won, 27-17.

An Atlanta Falcon makes a futile move on the L.A. Rams' running back Eric Dickerson, whom O. J. Simpson called "the best I've seen, and I mean ever"—including "the Juice" himself.

Always best in the clutch, Denver's John Elway barks signals to his team. Elway had to wait till the last two seasons of his stellar 16-year career to win the biggest of the big ones.

in 1987, he owned the career and single-game rushing records—16,726 yards and 275 yards, respectively—had caught 492 passes, and even thrown eight touchdown passes. He blocked like a barrel. Inside this iron man, however, beat a heart so warm that he was known as Sweetness. He was, perhaps, the running back of the century, but he would not see its end. Twelve years after retirement Payton was diagnosed with an incurable liver disorder; on November 1, 1999, at age 45, he died of cancer.

The Air Game. Since the advent of the forward pass, quarterbacks, receivers, pass rushers, and defensive backs have lived in uneasy symbiosis. The passer has about three seconds to unleash the ball before linemen and linebackers pile drive him to the turf. Downfield, pass catchers must negotiate the no-fly zones patrolled by tough, fast enforcers like Redskins cornerback Darrell Green *(inset)*.

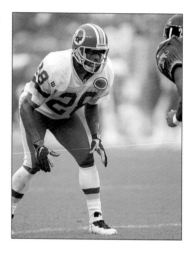

Quarterbacks John Elway *(left, top)* and Dan Marino *(left, bottom)* did it with consummate skill and poise. Marino's name appears all over the NFL record books. Among other career marks, he far exceeds anyone in league history in passes completed, yards gained passing, and touchdown passes. Yet with all that firepower his Dolphins have gone to only one Super Bowl, losing to the 49ers in 1985. What they had in artillery they lacked in defense and ground attack.

The 49ers were already a powerhouse, so it seemed unfair that they should be able to add Jerry Rice *(right, top)* to their arsenal. As great running with the ball as he was catching it, he set NFL career records for catches made and yards gained receiving, accumulating three Super Bowl rings in the process.

Out to destroy the air game are the great pass rushers. In 14 seasons at defensive end in the NFL, Reggie White *(far right)* totaled a record 192½ quarterback sacks. "I've been around a lot of great defensive linemen," said defensive coaching genius Buddy Ryan, "and Reggie's the best." Others might reserve that accolade for Buffalo's Bruce Smith *(right)*. A shade shorter and

The Miami Dolphins' Dan Marino cocks his steel-spring right arm, sorting out a crowd of moving targets. Holder of the NFL record for most and second most TD passes in a season, Marino was the first rookie quarterback to start in the Pro Bowl.

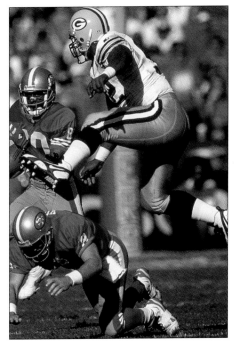

San Francisco's Jerry Rice (above) shows why many consider him the greatest receiver ever with this finger-tip catch against the Bengals in Super Bowl XXIII.

Buffalo Bills defensive end Bruce Smith (far left) goes mano a mano with a Houston Oilers lineman en route to a high-speed collision with the quarterback.

Green Bay's Reggie White (left), all-time NFL sack leader, vaults a would-be blocker in hot pursuit of number 80, Jerry Rice.

San Francisco quarterback Steve Young dives
past fallen Cowboys into the Dallas end zone
for a third-period touchdown in the 1995 NFC
play-off, a 38-28 49ers win.

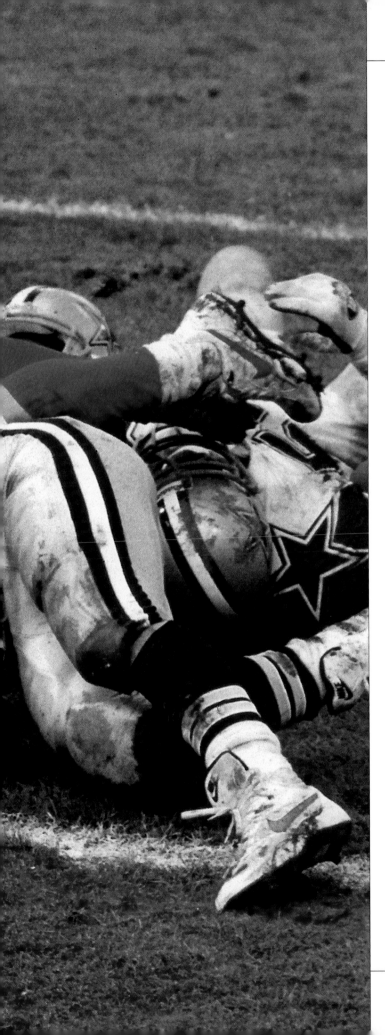

lighter than White, Smith was quicker, tearing around offensive lines to rank among the NFL's sack leaders 12 times.

An Array of Champions. At the start of the 1990s the Buffalo Bills, led by quarterback Jim Kelly, seemed destined to be the next dominant franchise. But in the 1991 Super Bowl they were undone by the phrase "wide right," which described the trajectory of a 47-yard Bills field goal try with eight seconds left and the Giants leading 20-19.

It was a portent. In all, Buffalo won the AFC title four years running—1991 through 1994—but failed every time in the Super Bowl. The Redskins took them down 37-24 in 1992. Then the Cowboys, back in the show for the first time since losing to Pittsburgh in 1979, routed them twice in 1993 and '94 with the starring duo of quarterback Troy Aikman and running back Emmitt Smith. Two years later, with the remarkable cornerback/showman Deion Sanders *(inset, page 162)* added to the mix, the Cowboys won their third Super Bowl in four years, beating the Steelers 27-17.

Between Cowboys victories, Joe Montana's outstanding successor, Steve Young *(left),* steered the 49ers to his first— and his team's record-breaking fifth—Super Bowl victory in 1995, bouncing the San Diego Chargers 49-26.

In the footsteps of the Cowboys and 'Niners came Green Bay, missing from Super Bowls since it won the first two. Its "cheesehead" fans cheered quarterback Brett Favre *(page 162, top)* and pass rusher Reggie White in Super Bowl XXXI, where the Pack blasted the New England Patriots 35-21. Green Bay returned the next year to face Denver in its seemingly annual Super Bowl appearance—number five after four haunting losses.

A Game for All Seasons. In 1983 Stanford's great quarterback John Elway was drafted number one by the Colts but refused to sign with them, disliking their coach. He threatened to play baseball instead, so the Colts relented and traded him to Denver. By 1986 he'd stolen an AFC title game from Cleveland when, with time running out, he launched a 98-yard drive to overcome a 20-13 deficit, eventually winning 23-20 in overtime. Back in the Super Bowl for the first time since a loss

Ringed by adoring fans, Packers quarterback Brett Favre savors Green Bay's victorious 1997 return to the Super Bowl after 29 years away.

Detroit's Barry Sanders picks up blockers in a 1994 run against Green Bay. Sanders was closing in on Walter Payton's career rushing record when he unexpectedly retired before the 1999 season.

nine years earlier, the Broncos were severely mistreated 39-20 by the Giants.

Back yet again the following year, Elway and the Broncos were humiliated by Doug Williams's formidable Redskins outfit, 42-10 *(page 154)*. Elway and his team tried one more time in 1990, only to be routed by the 49ers of Montana and Rice. Elway became, like Marino, a champion quarterback without a champion team.

By the time Super Bowl XXXII rolled around in 1998, the NFC had chalked up 13 consecutive victories, and if the oddsmakers were any guide, the Broncos, with the 37-year-old Elway at the helm, would not snap that streak. But after 56 minutes of play Denver was deadlocked with Brett Favre's Packers. Then Elway took affairs in hand, drawing upon his 16 years of expertise in clutch play. His brilliant young running back, Terrell Davis, capped off the Broncos' final drive with a TD run for the win, ending Denver's and Elway's dark age of frustration.

A year later, Elway *(page 158)* returned for the last Super Bowl of the millennium, against Atlanta. He was now aging, but again had a superb supporting cast. His once jinxed team prevailed 34-19. Elway retired after that season with the most fourth-quarter comebacks ever to his credit and, most important of all, two championship rings.

The makeup of the league Elway left was as different from the one he entered in 1983 as 1983 had been from Jim Thorpe's time. Some fans forgot that the Indianapolis Colts had once been the quintessential champions of Baltimore, which now fielded Cleveland's former team, renamed the Ravens. The Arizona Cardinals had made a long exodus from Chicago by way of St. Louis. The St. Louis Rams had earlier won championships in Cleveland, then Los Angeles. Mobility became almost as common for teams as for free agents, and new franchises popped up in sun-washed venues. Charlotte got the Carolina Panthers; Florida added the Jacksonville Jaguars; and a new Cleveland Browns team, with the history, traditions, and regalia of the old, reappeared on Lake Erie.

And yet the basic game remained the same. The Vikings' Randy Moss *(right)* would have been comfortable catching Sammy Baugh's passes, and a lateral from Thorpe to Detroit's brilliant runner Barry Sanders *(middle)* would have been as natural as a handshake. The money is better, the highly conditioned players bigger, stronger, and faster. But the addictive element in football—the excited rush of the scrimmage, the war fought in a 100-yard pressure cooker—has proved enduring.

Versatile Dallas cornerback and sometime outfielder Deion "Prime Time" Sanders is the only athlete who played in both the Super Bowl and World Series.

Wide receiver Randy Moss performs his trademark high-step end zone dance after a 51-yard pass play against Dallas in 1998, his first year with the Vikings.

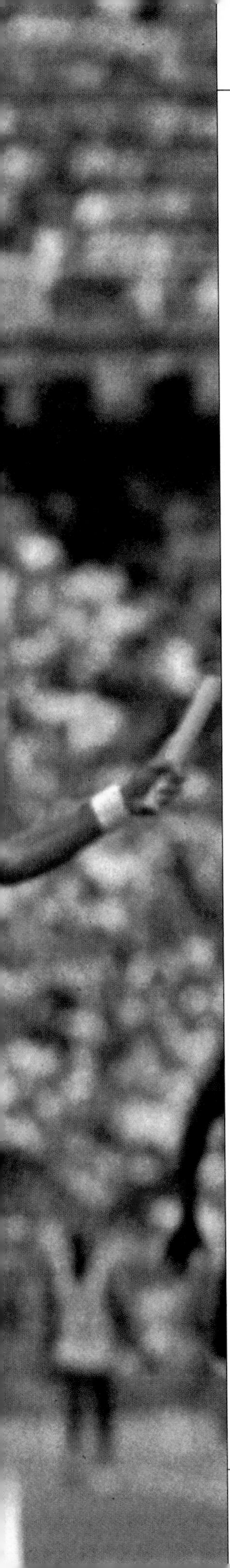

Americans on the World Stage

★

MORE THAN JUST A GAME

When Americans think of classic sports rivalries, the kinds of match-ups that usually come to mind—the Yankees and the Dodgers, say, or Ohio State against Michigan—are purely domestic. But some of the 20th century's biggest moments for U.S. athletes have played out in the international arena. The global spotlight always shines on the Olympics, of course, and on the highest levels of sports as popular as soccer, creating a worldwide audience for such moments as Brandi Chastain's burst of exultation *(inset)* when her successful penalty kick secured an American victory in the 1999 Women's World Cup.

But international sports are seldom without the weight of international relations, nor does the world often provide a setting free of tensions and tragedies in which athletes can play their games in peace. In 1936 Adolf Hitler tried to make the Berlin Olympics a triumph of Aryan racial superiority. When the Cold War locked the United States and the Soviet Union in a decades-long battle of nerves, the missile race and space race were joined every four years by the gold medal race.

But sports could also bring relief from politics, as athletes forged friendships across

An elated Carl Lewis (left) wins the gold for the United States in the 4 x 100-meter relay at the 1992 Barcelona Olympics. The silver and bronze medalists, from Nigeria and Cuba, give way to their own joy.

Jesse Owens accelerates down the track at the 1936 Olympics to win one of a record four gold medals and a permanent place in sports history.

ideological borders. And sometimes nations put aside antagonisms to pay tribute to superb athletic achievement, no matter by whom. At such moments sport ceased to be about rivalry and became a powerful, if short-lived, symbol of shared humanity.

Smashing the Aryan Myth. The 1936 Olympic Games opened in Berlin as a pageant of propaganda. Two years before Hitler's Nazi Party rose to power, Germany had been selected to host the 1936 Games. Now, with the eyes of the world turned his way, Hitler put on a lavish spectacle (right) meant also as a demonstration of Aryan supremacy.

About six weeks before the Games, German boxer Max Schmeling had knocked out African American heavyweight champion Joe Louis (page 87), and the regime hoped that its Olympic track-and-field team would provide a similar display of racial mastery. But the U.S. team included an Ohio State University student named Jesse Owens—born the son of Alabama share-croppers and the grandson of slaves. The previous year at the Big Ten track championships, Owens had achieved an astounding feat: In a single after-noon he set three world records and matched a fourth.

His performance in Berlin proved even more legendary. Owens collected three gold medals in as many days—winning the 100-meter dash, the broad jump, and the 200-meter dash—and then took a fourth gold with the U.S. 4 x 100-meter relay team. In every event he broke or tied a world or Olympic record. "Each time after I won," Owens later recalled, "I knew the incomparable thrill of seeing the American flag raised in the German stadium." In the face of Nazi racism, he also became friends with German athlete Luz Long, his competitor in the broad jump, who had even tipped Owens off on how to overcome a fouling problem.

Owens was welcomed back to the United States with a ticker-tape parade, but fame was no assurance of fortune for an African American athlete in the almost uni-formly racist American soci-ety of the time. For a while he could earn a living only by running exhibition

Banners emblazoned with swastikas loom over the opening ceremonies of the Berlin Olympics, as a torchbearer carries the Olympic flame past an audience that includes Adolf Hitler.

While Nazi salutes go up around him, Jesse Owens—crowned with the winner's wreath of laurel—gives his own American-style salute from the award stand.

races against horses. Eventually he found success as a businessman, public speaker, and sports commissioner. Owens's Olympic feat never faded from public memory, and in 1976, four years before his death, he was awarded the Presidential Medal of Freedom.

A Chilly New Beginning. War forced cancellation of the Olympics in 1940 and 1944, but the Games resumed in a London still bearing the scars of German bombing raids. Ostensibly a sign of the return of peace, the 1948 Games were marked by lingering hatreds and new enmities. The organizers did not invite former Axis powers Germany, Italy, and Japan, and Stalin's Soviet Union, increasingly hostile toward the West, refused to participate. That June, Soviet troops had cut off all surface access to the Western-occupied sectors of Berlin in an attempt to bring the entire city under Moscow's control. In response, British and American airplanes were flying in food, medicine, and fuel to keep West Berliners alive and defiant *(left)*.

Despite such tensions, a record 59 countries sent athletes to London that July and August to compete in unusually cold, wet weather. One of the youngest participants was 17-year-old Bob Mathias of California. Just a few months earlier Mathias's high-school coach had suggested that the track star take on a new challenge by competing in a decathlon—a grueling two-day, 10-event combination considered the ultimate test of athletic stamina, skill, and versatility. Mathias had never thrown a javelin, pole-vaulted, or run a 1,500-meter race, and his coach had to consult a manual to figure out how to train him in those events. Amazingly, though, the boy took first place in the U.S. Olympic trials that summer. Suddenly the plan was no longer to see if Mathias could compete in the Helsinki Olympics four years hence but to put him on a plane to London.

There Mathias lost points when his best shot put was disqualified after he exited the throwing circle incorrectly. On the second day officials could not locate the dent made by Mathias's longest discus toss *(right)* on the rain-soaked field, and the guess they made probably shortchanged him. Even so, by this point he had done well enough to move into the lead.

Night was now falling and the cold rain came down steadily as Mathias waited his turn for the three remaining events, which happened to be the ones he had learned only that spring: the pole vault, the javelin, and the 1,500 meters. He held his own in each. It was close to midnight when he staggered across the finish line of the 1,500, exhausted, to win the gold

A June 1948 headline predicts a grim fate for West Berlin under the Soviet blockade. But as residents look on, an American C-47 arrives with a load of dehydrated food. The Berlin airlift, which formed the political backdrop for the 1948 Olympics, lasted until May 1949, when the U.S.S.R. backed down and ended the blockade.

Bob Mathias, 17, hurls his discus at the 1948 London Olympics (opposite). His decathlon victory made him the youngest winner of a men's track-and-field event in Olympic history. He later played football for Stanford and won the decathlon again in the 1952 Games—becoming the first person to compete in the Olympics and the Rose Bowl in the same year.

RED 'MOON' PASSES OVER DETROIT TODAY

Speeds 18,000 MPH
560 Miles Over Earth

Arkansas Peace Formula Given to Ike, Faubus

"Whether you like it or not, history is on our side. We will bury you."

Nikita Khrushchev, 1956

Soviet leader Nikita Khrushchev gestures in the confrontational style that—like his 1957 launch of Sputnik—sharpened Cold War fears.

medal. Asked how he intended to celebrate, the teenager said, "I'll start shaving, I guess." His stunning achievement was no fluke: Four years later Mathias became history's first two-time gold medalist in the decathlon.

The Brotherhood of Sport. In 1958 an exceptional moment in sports history seemed to make the Cold War melt away temporarily. The timing was as unpropitious as could be imagined. In late 1957 the Soviets had launched Sputnik *(left)*, the first artificial satellite, and Soviet boss Nikita Khrushchev was making bellicose boasts about the U.S.S.R.'s growing might *(left, bottom)*. In this atmosphere of tension, Rafer Johnson, an African American college athlete, went to Moscow for a July 1958 U.S.-Soviet track meet. There he faced the formidable Vasily Kuznetsov, the Soviet "Man of Steel."

Johnson was no stranger to challenges. At age 10 he had suffered a mangled foot in an accident. The injury remained painful, but Johnson overcame it—as he did poverty and racism. In high school he was captain of the football, basketball, and track teams. He won an academic scholarship to UCLA and there became student body president.

But his true passion had been the decathlon, and in 1955 he broke Mathias's 1952 world record. He then competed in the 1956 Olympics but, injured, only won the silver medal. His world record still stood, however—until 10 weeks before the Moscow meet, when Kuznetsov broke it. Despite recent knee surgery, Johnson hoped to regain supremacy.

After the first day of competition, Johnson held a slight lead, though Kuznetsov was favored in the second day's events. But with the next-to-last event, the javelin throw, two extraordinary things happened: Johnson made a throw that was instantly recognizable as magnificent—and the 30,000 Russians packed into Lenin Stadium roared in response. The javelin traveled more than 238 feet, enough to set a new record point total for the decathlon—with one event still to go! The crowd—and Kuznetsov himself *(right)*—could not help but applaud this achievement, though it meant defeat for the national favorite.

Johnson was deeply moved: "Away from home, I have never seen spectators who seemed so proud of what I had done, and I was not one of their men." He ended the decathlon with a total of 8,302 points, a remarkable 405 points above Kuznetsov's record. Clustering around Johnson, the Russians tossed him into the air in celebration. A Moscow newspaper declared that his victory would "dignify the history of

Vasily Kuznetsov gives a European-style kiss of congratulation to victorious Rafer Johnson, the decathlon rival who had become his friend.

*Peggy Fleming takes a practice turn on the ice
as she prepares to capture the only U.S. gold
medal of the 1968 Winter Olympics. Her success
was one bright note in a troubled year.*

*Tommie Smith (left) and John Carlos raise black-
gloved fists at the 1968 Olympics, provoking out-
rage. But in a later sign of reconciliation,
they were among the torchbearers for
the 1996 Games.*

world athletic records for a long time to come." On this point, at least, the Soviets and Americans were in full agreement; *Sports Illustrated* somewhat exuberantly proclaimed Johnson "the finest all-round athlete in the history of mankind." He went on to win the gold medal at the 1960 Olympics.

Time of Turmoil. The '60s was a turbulent decade, and 1968 proved its most turbulent year. In January Communist forces in Vietnam launched the stunning Tet Offensive against U.S. troops, forcing America to confront the possibility of defeat. Assassins killed Martin Luther King in April and Robert Kennedy in June, plunging the nation into mourning. Riots tore apart American cities in the aftermath of King's death, then paralyzed Chicago in August during the Democratic National Convention, as protesters and police clashed. That same month Soviet troops invaded Czechoslovakia, crushing a short-lived experiment in liberalization behind the Iron Curtain.

For a time the world of sports offered some distraction from the tumult. The 1968 Winter Olympics in Grenoble, France, opened as the fighting raged in Vietnam, and for a few days the lovely image of 19-year-old figure skater Peggy Fleming *(left, top)* soothed the spirits of American viewers. With her balletic, lyrical style, she glided easily to a gold medal.

By contrast, the Summer Olympics, held in Mexico City that October, could not escape America's social conflicts. Some African American athletes, led by track star Tommie Smith, had called for a black boycott of the Games, arguing against representing a country that did not grant them full civil rights. The boycott movement never gathered steam, and Smith relented and went to Mexico. But his urge to make a statement about racism remained and led to one of modern sports history's most dramatic moments. In the 200-meter dash, Smith—ranked among the century's best American sprinters—raced to a first-place finish and a new world record. His teammate John Carlos won the bronze in the same event. When the two men took the victory stand, viewers around the world saw that they stood shoeless, to symbolize black poverty. Then "The Star-Spangled Banner" began, and the two men bowed their heads and raised a fist in the Black Power salute *(left)*.

Their gesture made them outcasts at the Games. Olympic officials expelled them immediately, and both men would suffer fallout from the event for years to come. Many viewers condemned their deed, but some athletes backed them. Among these were the silver medalist with them on the stand, Australian Peter Norman, and Bob Beamon, who left his own mark on history two days later with an astonishing long jump *(right)*. Like Smith and

At the Mexico City Olympics, long jumper Bob Beamon soars more than 29 feet through the air—almost two feet farther than anyone had ever jumped before—to set a record that stood until 1991.

A masked Palestinian terrorist emerges onto a balcony from the Munich apartment where Israeli athletes were held hostage during the 1972 Summer Olympics. The attack cost 11 Israeli lives—the worst tragedy in the history of the Games.

Carlos, Beamon wore black on the victory stand. Wyomia Tyus dedicated the gold medal she won in the 100-meter dash to the two men, later declaring, "What I did was win a track event. What they did lasted a lifetime, and life is bigger than sport."

Terror at the Games. After the tensions of 1968, it was hoped that politics would stay off the sports page during the 1972 Munich Olympics. And indeed, the Games' first 10 days were a celebration of sport, highlighted by the spectacular performance of American swimmer Mark Spitz *(left, bottom),* who, in seven events, piled up seven golds *(page 132).*

Then everything changed. Before dawn on September 5, eight Palestinian terrorists *(left)* stormed the Israeli team's quarters at the Olympic Village. They killed two team members and took nine hostage, demanding the release of 200 Arab prisoners from Israeli jails. After a 17-hour standoff, German authorities agreed to have a plane ready for the terrorists and their hostages at a nearby airfield. Waiting in ambush were German police sharpshooters, but their planned rescue failed disastrously. During a firefight the Palestinians killed all nine hostages.

The Games paused for a day, as 80,000 people gathered at a memorial service for the slain athletes. There officials announced, to some controversy, that competition would resume. Meanwhile, Israel and West Germany were both reeling. The murder of Jews on German soil contained grotesque echoes of the Holocaust, marring Germany's first post-1936 Olympics, an event meant to show the country's new, peaceful face.

Spirits were low as the Games resumed, but an American team encountered a twist of fate that, though it paled next to the terrorist tragedy, made things even worse. The Americans had won every gold medal—in fact, every game they ever played—in Olympic basketball history. This year the final match against the Soviet Union was expected to be another U.S. victory. But the Soviets played surprisingly tough, leading by as many as 10 points in the first half. The U.S. cut away at the lead and, with only three seconds left in the game, went ahead by a single point. A last-gasp Soviet shot missed, and the United States had apparently won the gold. But the Soviets argued that a time-out they requested had been ignored. Officials reset the clock to three seconds, but it ran out with no further scoring. Then, in a decision that unleashed fierce controversy, the British head of

Swimmer Mark Spitz poses with his seven gold medals. His victories made him an instant celebrity and provided a moment of triumph amid contention and violence.

American basketball players stand stunned (inset) as their Soviet opponents celebrate an amazing upset in 1972. The first U.S. basketball loss in the history of the Olympics—stemming from a series of hotly contested official decisions—proved a lingering sore spot.

Team captain Mike Eruzione's game-winning shot eludes the Soviet goalie and flies into the net, lifting American spirits in 1980.

the International Amateur Basketball Federation ordered the time put back on the clock yet again, and this time the Soviets scored and won. The Soviets celebrated as the American players stood in disbelief. The U.S. team protested vociferously, but the officials refused to budge. The bitter American players never accepted silver medals.

Miracle on Ice. As the 1980 Winter Olympics opened in Lake Placid, New York, American national morale was low. The economy was sagging into recession under the weight of inflation, unemployment, and an energy crisis. U.S. diplomats had been held hostage in Iran for almost four months. And just six weeks before the Games the Soviet Union invaded Afghanistan. President Jimmy Carter responded with trade sanctions against the U.S.S.R., and headlines *(inset)* proclaimed his plan to boycott the upcoming Summer Olympics in Moscow unless the Soviets withdrew their troops by February 20. The deadline came and went with no Soviet response, dooming U.S. athletes' hopes of competing in Moscow. Meanwhile, the

Winter Games at Lake Placid began, but they too seemed starcrossed—a poorly run transportation system stranded thousands of angry ticket holders who never made it to events.

On February 22, just two days after Carter's deadline, the U.S. and U.S.S.R. hockey teams were scheduled to face off. The Americans were an unheralded collection of college kids. The high-powered, state-supported Soviet team, ranked number one in the world, had decimated the National Hockey League all-stars the year before and thrashed the U.S. squad in an exhibition game a few days before the Olympics began. The outcome seemed inevitable.

But after two tightly played periods, the Soviets led by just one goal. Midway through the final period—as the mostly American crowd chanted "USA! USA!"—the Americans drove two pucks past the Soviet goalie in a space of just over a minute to take a 4-3 lead *(left)*. Delirious spectators rose to their feet and stayed there, waving their American flags, for the 10 excruciatingly long minutes left in the game. The Soviets launched a frenzied assault against U.S. goalie Jim Craig, but he turned away shot after shot. As the final seconds ticked down, broadcaster Al Michaels shouted, "Do you believe in miracles?" and the crowd exploded in celebration—along

with the rest of the country. For Americans, this upset victory over a Cold War rival meant more than just a hockey win—more even than the gold medal the U.S. team would win two days later with a 4-2 over Finland. It was a moment of patriotic pride and renewed optimism in the middle of a dark winter.

When Worlds Collide. Controversy swirled around the 1984 Summer Olympics in Los Angeles even before it began. First there was the boycott by the Soviet bloc teams—except for Romania—in retaliation for the U.S. boycott of the 1980 Games in Moscow. Then there was the upcoming showdown between two track stars—the U.S. favorite, Mary Decker, and Zola Budd, a South African teenager who, according to some, should not have been allowed into the Olympics at all.

Decker, 26, was the best female middle-distance runner in the United States, possibly in the world. By late 1983 she held the American or world record in every event from 800 to 10,000 meters. But although she had been running competitively since age 11, she had never made it to an Olympics. In 1972 she was too young. She was sidelined by injury in 1976 and was a casualty of the boycott in 1980. It looked like 1984 would finally be her year.

Budd came to international attention only that January, when, at age 17, she shattered the 5,000-meter record that Decker, her idol, had set. Now the shy, 84-pound girl, who grew up running barefoot across the hills of South Africa, found herself vilified for her country's hated policy of apartheid. Budd had taken British citizenship that spring, thereby circumventing the worldwide ban on South African participation in international sports events. But antiapartheid protesters greeted her at every turn in Britain, and for a time it seemed that there might be a widespread boycott of the Games by African nations if she were allowed to participate. In the eye of the storm Budd pleaded for sympathy: "I'm not a politician, I'm just a girl who wants to run."

The two athletes went head to head in the 3,000-meter run. Decker, as expected, led from the outset, but with three laps remaining, Budd moved in front (left). Decker tried to repass, and the two made contact. Their legs tangled, and Decker plunged to the infield grass (right), pulling a muscle. She lay writhing and screaming in pain, grief, and rage, unable to rise again.

Budd somehow regained her balance and continued to run, but in tears, as the crowd booed her mercilessly. She finished seventh. Immediately after the race, with her ankle still bleeding from the collision, she sought out Decker to apologize. "Don't bother," Decker snapped. Officials at first disqualified Budd, then after viewing tapes reversed the decision, declaring neither athlete was at fault. After receiving death threats, Budd needed police

Moments after South African-born Zola Budd passes U.S. runner Mary Decker (opposite) at the 1984 Olympics, disaster ensues. Without enough space between them, Decker comes down on Budd's bare foot. Budd's leg inadvertently flies out, and Decker trips (top). The American tumbles off the track (middle), as Budd looks back in shock (above).

Romanian gymnast Ecaterina Szabo keeps a poker face as Mary Lou Retton posts a perfect 10.

protection for her trip back to England. There she continued to be taunted. Within four years she moved back to South Africa following a near nervous breakdown. Instead of Olympic glory, and despite their other magnificent accomplishments, both Decker and Budd found themselves remembered most for that awful moment in Los Angeles.

Unexpected Perfection. Up to 1984 no American woman had ever won an individual Olympic gymnastics medal. Even that year, with the traditionally powerful Soviet bloc teams boycotting the Los Angeles Games, American hopes were not high. The favorite was reigning world champion Ecaterina Szabo of Romania *(left)*. The leading American contestant, 16-year-old Mary Lou Retton *(opposite, top)*, had never taken part in a major international competition.

But when Retton and Szabo sized each other up, the American remarked, "What she doesn't know about me is that I'm tougher than she is." The 4-foot-9-inch, 92-pound Retton represented a new style of gymnast, one who combined grace with power and daring. Along with her fierce

Szabo whirls to her own perfect 10 on the balance beam as she strives for the individual all-around gymnastics gold medal at the 1984 Games.

determination, she displayed high spirits and an irresistible grin, qualities that would make her a hit with the public.

Just the year before, Retton's family had let her move from their home in West Virginia to Houston, so that she could train under legendary coach Bela Karolyi. Karolyi knew a potential champion when he saw one, saying, "She's got the psychological power to go through the most difficult moments without falling apart." That power got a test less than six weeks before the Olympics, when Retton's right knee suddenly seized. A doctor told her that competition was out of the question, but one day after arthroscopic surgery to remove torn cartilage from her knee she was back in the gym working out.

The contest for the individual all-around gold medal turned into a dramatic showdown between Szabo and Retton. Retton had an early, razor-thin lead, but then the advantage shifted to Szabo. She scored a perfect 10 on the balance beam with four stunning consecutive back handsprings *(left, bottom),* nearly matched Retton's 10 in the floor exercises, and outshone her on the uneven bars.

Taut, strong, and fearless, Mary Lou Retton shows a face ready for any challenge.

Retton takes the gold medal with a flawless vault, declaring afterward, "I vault best under pressure. It makes me fight harder."

Wearing the yellow shirt of the race leader, Greg LeMond rolls to victory in the 1986 Tour de France.

Retton, preparing for her vault, knew she needed another perfect score to win. What she planned was a layout back somersault with a double twist, a vault no other woman could perform. She executed it flawlessly *(page 181)*—and the 10 went up on the scoreboard. Later, with the gold medal around her neck, Retton bubbled, "Well, nobody thought it could be done. But you know what? I went and *did* it."

An American Takes Paris. The Tour de France, the world's premier bicycle race, had been a European preserve for some 80 years when American Greg LeMond entered it in 1984. Only one American before him had even tried the event, and no non-European had ever won it.

Four years earlier, LeMond was captain of the U.S. Olympic cycling team, but after the boycott of the 1980 Moscow Games he moved to Europe, turned professional, and learned the intricacies of team racing. Each team selects its lead racer in advance. Teammates help him by setting a pace and by surging ahead to ease wind resistance for him and box in or wear down other riders. This contest of split-second coordination and chesslike strategy lasts three weeks, up and down 2,500 miles of rolling countryside and steep mountains.

LeMond placed third in the 1984 Tour. The next year he came in second to his La Vie Claire teammate Bernard Hinault, who then proclaimed that 1986 would be LeMond's turn to win. At age 31, Hinault had a record-tying five championships and said he was ready to retire. But as the 1986 race unfolded, it became clear that Hinault was in fact going for first place, meanwhile doing his best to wear LeMond down. LeMond pressed ahead grimly.

At one point, a fall seemed to doom his chances. But at the end of that leg Hinault, strangely, declared that his rough tactics had only been meant to get the best from LeMond, and he began supporting LeMond's ride. Three days later LeMond stunned France and all of Europe—and made himself an American hero—by rolling across the finish line in Paris in first place *(left),* about three minutes ahead of Hinault.

As towering as LeMond's achievement was, he would soon face even greater challenges. A hunting accident in

Ben Johnson sprinted to a spectacular victory in the 1988 Olympics, only to take a spectacular fall—stripped of his medal for steroid use.

The 1988 bombing of Pan Am Flight 103 showed that not all threats waned with the Cold War. Terrorism prompted new fears—as did AIDS.

1987 left him with 30 lead pellets in his body, including two in the lining of his heart. Yet he staged an incredible comeback to win the Tour a second time in 1989—by eight seconds, the smallest margin ever—and then again in 1990.

Medical Perils. No one could have guessed that the 1988 Olympics, in Seoul, would be the last Games to be tainted by the U.S.-Soviet rivalry. But though Cold War tensions were already easing, other dangers loomed. In late 1988 the bomb that destroyed Pan Am Flight 103 over Lockerbie, Scotland *(left, bottom)*, made terrorism the fresh stuff of nightmares. And the menace of HIV/AIDS was spreading fear, misery, and death.

Celebrated American diver Greg Louganis tested positive for the AIDS virus six months before the 1988 Olympics, at a time when an HIV diagnosis could mean social ostracism. He told few people beyond his doctor and his coach. Then, in a preliminary dive at the Games, he struck his head on the board. Though experts assured him later that blood from the gash on his head posed no risk to others who were in the pool when he fell, and little risk to the doctor who closed the wound, he faced a horrible dilemma. Should he withdraw from the competition, which would almost certainly lead to revelation of his awful secret? Or should he continue diving, which might eventually expose him to condemnation for knowingly putting others in jeopardy, no matter how slight the risk was? But Louganis was no quitter. He decided to return to the competition *(right)* and became the first man to achieve a "double double"—gold medals in both the springboard and diving events in successive Olympic Games. Louganis made his secret public in 1995. By now he had developed AIDS. His goal, he said, was to show others that even with the disease "you can have a career, have a life."

Another athlete at the Seoul Games had a medical secret of a different sort. Three days after Canadian sprinter Ben Johnson roared to a world-record time to win the 100-meter dash, officials stripped him of his gold medal and awarded it to runner-up Carl Lewis. Routine postrace tests had turned up evidence of anabolic steroid use *(left, top)*. Johnson at first denied using the dangerous drugs but later

At the Seoul Games, Greg Louganis demonstrates the soaring grace that made him the world's greatest diver. He won his second pair of gold medals just months after learning he was HIV positive.

confessed to years of illegal doping. Although the scandal was a black eye for the Games, many hoped it would keep other athletes from taking the same risks with their health and careers.

U.S. Women Triumph. In the 1990s a determined group of American women built themselves into a world power in soccer. In 1991 they won the first-ever Women's World Cup. At the 1996 Olympics, the first to include women's soccer, they bested a tough, highly disciplined Chinese team for the gold medal. And in the 1999 World Cup, after defeating Germany and Brazil in close contests, the U.S. team again faced China in the final game.

The American women had captured the country's imagination, and their match-up against the favored Chinese would occur against a background of testy China-U.S. relations, adding to the

drama. More than 90,000 spectators jammed Pasadena's Rose Bowl for the game—the largest crowd ever at an all-female sporting event —and 40 million followed it on TV. The two teams battled in the southern California heat for 90 minutes, neither able to score. The game went through one 15-minute overtime, then another, still scoreless.

As the suspense peaked, the teams faced off for a final duel of penalty kicks, five per team. "I knew I just had to make one save," U.S. goalie Briana Scurry said, "because I knew my teammates would make their shots." Scurry punched away the third Chinese kick with an astonishing lunging dive. When Brandi Chastain knocked in the final U.S. shot *(inset)* to win the shootout 5-4, she snatched off her shirt in her excitement as a torrent of emotion poured forth from the team—what Chastain described as "elation, utter craziness, insanity" *(right)*. The U.S. players had added new names to the roster of American sports heroes—Michelle Akers, Mia Hamm, Joy Fawcett—and they had lifted both soccer and women's sports to a new level of national prominence.

As Brandi Chastain's penalty kick plunges into the net (in the opposite), the U.S. soccer team erupts in joy over its victory in the 1999 World Cup. "I just thought: This is the greatest moment of my life on a soccer field," Chastain said.

ACKNOWLEDGMENTS

The editors wish to thank the following individuals and institutions for their valuable assistance in the preparation of this volume:
Joe Amati, NBA Photos, Secaucus, N.J.; James Beck, A. J.'s Sport Stop, Vienna, Va.; Frank Deford, *Sports Illustrated*, New York; Mary Ison and Staff, Library of Congress, Washington, D.C.; Jerry Kirshenbaum, New York; Paul Spinelli, NFL Properties, Inc., Los Angeles; Milo Stewart Jr., National Baseball Hall of Fame Library, Cooperstown, N.Y.; Bob Sullivan, *Life* Magazine, New York; Marlene Wasikowski, University of Notre Dame Photo Archives, Notre Dame, Ind.

BIBLIOGRAPHY

BOOKS

African American Biography: Vol. 2. Detroit: Gale Research, 1994.

American Decades (selected volumes, 1920-1989). Detroit: Gale Research, 1994-1996.

Anderson, Dave:
> *The Story of Basketball*. New York: William Morrow, 1988.
> *The Story of Football*. New York: Beech Tree Books, 1985.

Atlanta 1996: Official Publication of the U.S. Olympic Committee. Salt Lake City: Commemorative Publications, 1996.

Barber, Phil, and Ray Didinger. *Football America*. Atlanta: Turner Publishing, 1996.

The Baseball Anthology. New York: Harry N. Abrams, 1994.

The Baseball Encyclopedia. New York: Macmillan, 1996.

Bjarkman, Peter C. *Hoopla: A Century of College Basketball*. Indianapolis: Masters Press, 1996.

Bryant, Beverley. *Portraits in Roses: 108 Years of Kentucky Derby Winners*. New York: McGraw-Hill, 1984.

Bunce, Steve. *Boxing Greats*. Philadelphia: Courage Books, 1998.

Carter, Craig, ed. *Complete Baseball Record Book*. St. Louis: Sporting News, 1997.

Center, Bill, and Bob Moore. *NASCAR: 50 Greatest Drivers*. New York: HarperHorizon, 1998.

Chadwick, Bruce. *When the Game Was Black and White: The Illustrated History of the Negro Leagues*. New York: Abbeville Press, 1992.

Coffey, Wayne. *Wilma Rudolph*. Woodbridge, Conn.: Blackbirch Press, 1993.

Collins, Douglas. *Olympic Dreams: 100 Years of Excellence*. New York: Universe, 1996.

Condor, Bob. *Michael Jordan's 50 Greatest Games: From His NCAA Championship to Six NBA Titles*. Secaucus, N.J.: Carol Publishing Group, 1998.

Daly, Chuck, and Alex Sachare. *America's Dream Team: The Quest for Olympic Gold*. Atlanta: Turner Publishing, 1992.

Daly, Dan, and Bob O'Donnell. *The Pro Football Chronicle*. New York: Collier Books/Macmillan, 1990.

Douchant, Mike. *Encyclopedia of College Basketball*. New York: Gale Research, 1995.

Durant, John, and Otto Bettmann. *Pictorial History of American Sports*. New York: A. S. Barnes and Co., 1965.

ESPN SportsCentury. New York: Hyperion, 1999.

Glory and the Games. Salt Lake City: Commemorative Publications, 1998.

Golf: The Greatest Game. New York: HarperCollins, 1994.

Golf in America: The First One Hundred Years. New York: Harry N. Abrams, 1988.

Green, Jerry. *Super Bowl Chronicles*. Indianapolis: Masters Press, 1995.

Greenspan, Bud:
> *Frozen in Time: The Greatest Moments at the Winter Olympics*. Los Angeles: General Publishing Group, 1997.
> *100 Greatest Moments in Olympic History*. Los Angeles: General Publishing Group, 1995.

Gutman, Bill. *Shooting Stars: The Women of Pro Basketball*. New York: Random House, 1998.

Hickok, Ralph. *The Encyclopedia of North American Sports History*. New York: Facts On File, 1992.

Hunter, Don, and Ben White. *American Stock Car Racers*. Osceola, Wis.: Motorbooks International, 1997.

Iooss, Walter. *Walter Iooss: A Lifetime Shooting Sports & Beauty*. New York: Graphis, 1998.

James, Bill. *The Bill James Historical Baseball Abstract*. New York: Villard Books, 1986.

Johnson, Anne Janette. *Great Women in Sports*. Detroit: Visible Ink Press, 1996.

Johnson, Rafer. *The Best That I Can Be: An Autobiography*. New York: Doubleday, 1998.

Kahn, Roger. *The Era, 1947-1957: When the Yankees, the Giants, and the Dodgers Ruled the World*. New York: Ticknor & Fields, 1993.

Kalinsky, George. *The New York Knicks: The Official Fiftieth Anniversary Celebration*. New York: Macmillan, 1996.

Kavanagh, Jack, and James Tackach. *Great Athletes of the 20th Century*. New York: Gallery Books, 1989.

Knapp, Ron. *Top 10 Basketball Scorers*. Hillside, N.J.: Enslow Publishers, 1994.

Lawson, Gerald. *World Record Breakers in Track & Field Athletics*. Champaign, Ill.: Human Kinetics, 1997.

Layden, Joe. *Women in Sports*. Los Angeles: General Publishing Group, 1997.

Lincoln Library of Sports Champions. Columbus, Ohio: Frontier Press, 1989.

Lipofsky, Steve. *Bird: Portrait of a Competitor*. Lenexa, Kans.: Addax Publishing Group, 1998.

Lipsyte, Robert, and Peter Levine. *Idols of the Game*. Atlanta: Turner Publishing, 1995.

McDonough, Will, et al. *75 Seasons: The Complete Story of the National Football League, 1920-1995*. Atlanta: Turner Publishing, 1994.

McMane, Fred. *Superstars of Men's Track and Field*. Philadelphia: Chelsea House Publishers, 1998.

Mikan, George L., and Joseph Oberle. *Unstoppable: The Story of George Mikan, the First NBA Superstar*. Indianapolis: Masters Press, 1997.

Miller, J. David. *The Super Book of Football*. New York: *Sports Illustrated for Kids* Books, 1990.

Molzahn, Arlene Bourgeois. *Top 10 American Women Sprinters*. Springfield, N.J.: Enslow Publishers, 1998.

Myler, Patrick. *A Century of Boxing Greats*. Parkwest, N.Y.: Robson Books, 1997.

The NBA at 50. Ed. by Mark Vancil. Avenel, N.J.: Park Lane Press, 1996.

Nemec, David, et al. *Players of Cooperstown: Baseball's Hall of Fame*. Lincolnwood, Ill.: Publications International, 1998.

Oates, Joyce Carol. *On Boxing*. Hopewell, N.J.: Ecco Press, 1994.

Official 1999 National Football League Record & Fact Book. New York: Workman, 1999.

Orr, Jack. *The Black Athlete: His Story in American History*. New York: Lion Press, 1969.

Owens, Jesse, and Paul G. Neimark. *The Jesse Owens Story*. New York: G. P. Putnam's Sons, 1970.

Peper, George. *The Story of Golf*. New York: TV Books, 1999.

Peterson, Robert W. *Pigskin: The Early Years of Pro Football*. New York: Oxford University Press, 1997.

Rader, Benjamin G. *American Sports: From the Age of Folk Games to the Age of Televised Sports*. Englewood Cliffs, N.J.: Prentice Hall, 1996.

Reichler, Joseph, and Jack Clary. *Baseball's Great Moments*. New York: Galahad Books, 1990.

Roberts, James B., and Alexander G. Skutt. *The Boxing Register*. Ithaca, N.Y.: McBooks Press, 1999.

Shimabukuro, Mark. *The Sporting News Official Baseball Register*. St. Louis: Sporting News, 1994.

Siddons, Larry. *The Olympics at 100*. New York: Macmillan, 1995.

Smith, Ron. *The Sporting News Selects Football's Greatest Players: A Celebration of the 20th Century's Best*. Ed. by Carl Moritz. St. Louis: Sporting News, 1999.

Stravinsky, John. *Muhammad Ali*. New York: Park Lane Press, 1997.

Summerall, Pat. *Pat Summerall's Sports in America*. New York: HarperCollins, 1996.

Tennis (Vol. 6 of *The New York Times Encyclopedia of Sports*). Ed. by Gene Brown. New York: Arno Press, 1979.

Thorn, John. *Treasures of the Baseball Hall of Fame*. New York: Villard, 1998.

Thorn, John, et al., eds. *Total Baseball*. New York: Viking, 1997.

Ward, Geoffrey C. *Baseball: An Illustrated History*. New York: Alfred A. Knopf, 1994.

Wels, Susan. *The Olympic Spirit*. Del Mar, Calif.: Tehabi Books, 1996.

The Women's Sports Encyclopedia. New York: Henry Holt, 1997.

Woolum, Janet. *Outstanding Women Athletes*. Phoenix: Oryx Press, 1998.

PERIODICALS

Abt, Samuel. "American Victor Finds All Paris at His Feet." *New York Times*, July 26, 1999.

Akers, Michelle. "Olympic Mettle." *People*, November 10, 1997.

"American Athletes Sweep the Olympics." *Life*, August 23, 1948.

Brofman, Rob. "One for the Angels." *Life*, June 1989.

"A Champion Proves They Can Come Back." *Life*, January 23, 1950.

Chass, Murray. "In Baseball, October Goes to the Highest of the Bidders." *New York Times*, November 10, 1999.

Clarey, Christopher. "Triumphs Beyond First Place in the Hurdles." *New York Times*, August 20, 1999.

"Eddie Robinson Gets Heartfelt Farewell As He Retires After 56 Years." *Jet*, December 15, 1997.

Gildea, William. "Nation Mourns DiMaggio." *Washington Post*, March 9, 1999.

Goff, Steven. "Akers's Gritty Play Proves Inspirational to U.S. Squad." *Washington Post*, July 11, 1999.

"Grace Under Pressure." *Life*, April 1995.

McDermott, John R. "The Smiling Olympians." *Life*, February 23, 1968.

"Moscow's Hero." *Time*, August 11, 1958.

"Olympic Games." *Time*, August 17, 1936.

"The Robinsons and the La Mottas Go to a Great Fight." *Life*, February 26, 1951.

Sampras, Pete. "Lesson of the Heart." *People*, July 8, 1996.

Shapiro, Leonard. "NFL Legend Payton Dies." *Washington Post*, November 2, 1999.

"Soccer's Happiest Feat." *People*, July 26, 1999.

Sports Illustrated, August 16, 1954-December 13, 1999.

Starr, Mark, and Martha Brant. "Girls Rule!: Inside the Amazing World Cup Victory." *Newsweek*, July 19, 1999.

Sullivan, Robert. "Love Is a Reason to Live." *Life*, October 1997.

"Terror in the Night." *Time*, January 2, 1989.

"Tour de Force: Lance Armstrong Caps a Win Over Cancer With Victory in the World's Greatest Bike Race." *People*, August 9, 1999.

"Trials & Tryouts." *Time*, July 20, 1936.

OTHER SOURCES

"CBS Sportsline." Available: http://cbssportsline.com/ December 13, 1999.

"CNN/Sports Illustrated." Available: http://cnnsi.com/ December 13, 1999.

"espn.com." Available: http://espn.go.com/ December 13, 1999.

"The FIFA WWC '99 Official Program." 1999 Women's World Cup event program, June 19-July 10, 1999.

"Home Run Record." Available: http://www.homerunrecord.com/ December 13, 1999.

"majorleaguebaseball.com: The Official Site of Major League Baseball." Available: http://www.majorleaguebaseball.com/ December 13, 1999.

"NBA History." Available: http://nba.com/history/index.html December 6, 1999.

"NBA.com: The Official Site of the National Basketball Association." Available: http://nba.com/ December 13, 1999.

"NFL.com: The Official Site of the National Football League." Available: http://www.nfl.com/ December 13, 1999.

"NFL History: Exhaustive Expository Concordance of the NFL." Available: http://www.nflhistory.com/ December 14, 1999.

Pro Football Hall of Fame. Available: http://profootballhof.com/ December 14, 1999.

Scully, Vin, "29,000 people and a million butterflies" (transcript of radio program broadcast September 9, 1965), Salon People. Available: http://www.salon.com/people/feature/1999/10/12/scully_koufax/index.html December 13, 1999.

"SI Online." Available: http://cnnsi.com/si_online/index.html December 13, 1999.

"The Sporting News." Available: http://www.sportingnews.com/ December 13, 1999.

"Top N. American Athletes of the Century." Available: http://espn.go.com/sportscentury/athletes.html December 13, 1999.

"Total Baseball Online." Available: http://www.totalbaseball.com/ December 13, 1999.

INDEX

TIME®
LIFE
BOOKS

Time-Life Books is a division of Time Life Inc.

TIME LIFE INC.
CHAIRMAN AND CHIEF EXECUTIVE OFFICER: Jim Nelson
PRESIDENT AND CHIEF OPERATING OFFICER:
Steven Janas
SENIOR EXECUTIVE VICE PRESIDENT AND
CHIEF OPERATIONS OFFICER: Mary Davis Holt
SENIOR VICE PRESIDENT AND
CHIEF FINANCIAL OFFICER: Christopher Hearing

TIME-LIFE BOOKS
PRESIDENT: Joseph A. Kuna
PUBLISHER/MANAGING EDITOR: Neil Kagan
VICE PRESIDENT, NEW PRODUCT DEVELOPMENT:
Amy Golden

OUR AMERICAN CENTURY
A Century of Sports

EDITORS: Loretta Britten, Paul Mathless
Deputy Editor: Charles J. Hagner
Text Editor: Elizabeth Hedstrom
Associate Editor/Research and Writing: Ruth Goldberg
Senior Copyeditor: Judith Klein
Picture Associate: Anne Whittle
Technical Art Specialist: John Drummond
Editorial Assistant: Christine Higgins
Photo Coordinator: Betty H. Weatherley

Design for **Our American Century** by Antonio Alcalá,
Studio A, Alexandria, Virginia

Special Contributors: Edward Moser, Roger Williams (editing);
Reade Bailey, Ronald H. Bailey, Constance Buchanan, Christopher
Kinney, John Newton, Carl Posey, Henry Wiencek (writing);
Charlotte Fullerton, Victoria Garrett Jones, Dan Kulpinski, Corinna
Luyken, Jane Martin, Joan Mathys, Marilyn Terrell (research);
Richard Friend, Marti Davila (design); Susan Nedrow (index)

Correspondents: Maria Vincenza Aloisi (Paris), Christine Hinze
(London), Christina Lieberman (New York)

Separations by the Time-Life Imaging Department

NEW PRODUCT DEVELOPMENT: Director, Elizabeth D. Ward
MARKETING: Director, Pamela R. Farrell; Associate Marketing
Manager, Terri Miller

Senior Vice President, Law & Business Affairs: Randolph H. Elkins
Vice President, Finance: Claudia Goldberg
Vice President, Book Production: Patricia Pascale
Vice President, Imaging: Marjann Caldwell
Director, Publishing Technology: Betsi McGrath
Director, Editorial Administration: Barbara Levitt
Director, Photography and Research: John Conrad Weiser
Director, Quality Assurance: James King
Manager, Technical Services: Anne Topp
Senior Production Manager: Ken Sabol
Manager, Copyedit/Page Makeup: Debby Tait
Production Manager: Virginia Reardon
Chief Librarian: Louise D. Forstall

EDITORIAL CONSULTANT
Richard B. Stolley is currently senior editorial adviser at Time Inc.
After 19 years at *Life* magazine as a reporter, bureau chief, and
assistant managing editor, he became the first managing editor of
People magazine, a position he held with great success for eight
years. He then returned to *Life* magazine as managing editor and
later served as editorial director for all Time Inc. magazines. In
1997 Stolley received the Henry Johnson Fisher Award for
Lifetime Achievement, the magazine industry's highest honor.

Library of Congress Cataloging-in-Publication Data
A century of sports / by the editors of Time-Life Books; with a
foreword by Walter Iooss Jr.
p. cm. — (Our American century)
Includes bibliographical references (p.) and index.
ISBN 0-7835-5519-9
1. Sports—United States—History—20th century.
I. Time-Life Books. II. Series.
GV583 . A2   2000
796'.0973—dc21   99-059370
                                                            CIP

10 9 8 7 6 5 4 3 2 1

Other History Publications:
World War II   Lost Civilizations
What Life Was Like   Mysteries of the Unknown
The American Story   Time Frame
Voices of the Civil War   The Civil War
The American Indians   Cultural Atlas

For information on and a full description of any of the Time-
Life Books series listed above, please call 1-800-621-7026 or write:

Reader Information
Time-Life Customer Service
P.O. Box C-32068
Richmond, Virginia 23261-2068

*On the cover: Michael Jordan slices through the air for a lay-up
against Seattle in the 1996 NBA finals, as he leads the Chicago
Bulls to the fourth of their six championships in the 1990s. Each
championship brought Jordan a Most Valuable Player award—and
added further luster to his status as the greatest basketball player of
all time. Pictured from left to right at the top: baseball immortal
Babe Ruth; Hall of Fame quarterback Terry Bradshaw; tennis great
and women's sports trailblazer Billie Jean King; swimmer Matt
Biondi; champion sprinter Florence Griffith-Joyner; and golf jugger-
naut Tiger Woods. On the spine is peerless boxer Muhammad Ali.*